Your Personal Horoscope 2008

Taurus

GW00546751

YOUR PERSONAL HOROSCOPE 2008

TAURUS

21st April–21st May

igloo

igloo

This edition published by Igloo Books Ltd,
Cottage Farm, Mears Ashby Road, Sywell, Northants NN6 0BJ
www.igloo-books.com
E-mail: Info@igloo-books.com

Produced for Igloo Books by W. Foulsham & Co. Ltd,
The Publishing House, Bennetts Close, Cippenham,
Slough, Berkshire SL1 5AP, England

ISBN: 978-1-845-61620-5

This is an abridged version of material
originally published in *Old Moore's Horoscope
and Astral Diary*.

Printed in China

CONTENTS

CONTENTS

INTRODUCTION

Your Personal Horoscopes have been specifically created to allow you to get the most from astrological patterns and the way they have a bearing on not only your zodiac sign, but nuances within it. Using the diary section of the book you can read about the influences and possibilities of each and every day of the year. It will be possible for you to see when you are likely to be cheerful and happy or those times when your nature is in retreat and you will be more circumspect. The diary will help to give you a feel for the specific 'cycles' of astrology and the way they can subtly change your day-to-day life. For example, when you see the sign ☿, this means that the planet Mercury is retrograde at that time. Retrograde means it appears to be running backwards through the zodiac. Such a happening has a significant effect on communication skills, but this is only one small aspect of how the Personal Horoscope can help you.

With Your Personal Horoscope the story doesn't end with the diary pages. It includes simple ways for you to work out the zodiac sign the Moon occupied at the time of your birth, and what this means for your personality. In addition, if you know the time of day you were born, it is possible to discover your Ascendant, yet another important guide to your personal make-up and potential.

Many readers are interested in relationships and in knowing how well they get on with people of other astrological signs. You might also be interested in the way you appear to very different sorts of individuals. If you are such a person, the section on Venus will be of particular interest. Despite the rapidly changing position of this planet, you can work out your Venus sign, and learn what bearing it will have on your life.

Using Your Personal Horoscope you can travel on one of the most fascinating and rewarding journeys that anyone can take – the journey to a better realisation of self.

THE ESSENCE OF TAURUS

Exploring the Personality of Taurus the Bull

(21ST APRIL – 21ST MAY)

What's in a sign?

Taurus is probably one of the most misunderstood signs of the zodiac. Astrologers from the past described those born under the sign of the Bull as being gentle, artistic, stubborn and refined. All of this is quite true, but there is so much more to Taureans and the only reason it isn't always discussed as much as it should be is because of basic Taurean reserve. Taureans are generally modest, and don't tend to assert themselves in a direct sense, unless in self-defence. As a result the sign is often sidelined, if not ignored.

You know what you want from life and are quite willing to work long and hard to get it. However, Taurus is also a great lover of luxury, so when circumstances permit you can be slow, ponderous and even lax. If there is a paradox here it is merely typical of Venus-ruled Taurus. On differing occasions you can be chatty or quiet, bold or timorous, smart or scruffy. It all depends on your commitment to a situation. When you are inspired there is nobody powerful enough to hold you back and when you are passionate you have the proclivities of a Casanova!

There are aspects of your nature that seldom change. For example, you are almost always friendly and approachable, and invariably have a sense of what feels and looks just right. You are capable and can work with your hands as well as your brain. You don't particularly care for dirt or squalid surroundings, preferring cleanliness, and you certainly don't take kindly to abject poverty. Most Taureans prefer the country to the coast, find loving relationships easy to deal with and are quite committed to home and family.

Whilst variety is the spice of life to many zodiac signs this is not necessarily the case for Taurus. Many people born under the sign of the Bull remain happy to occupy a specific position for years on end.

It has been suggested, with more than a grain of truth, that the only thing that can get the Bull moving on occasions is a strategically placed bomb. What matters most, and which shows regularly in your dealings with the world at large, is your innate kindness and your desire to help others.

Taurus resources

The best word to describe Taurean subjects who are working to the best of their ability would be 'practical'. Nebulous situations, where you have to spend long hours thinking things through in a subconscious manner, don't suit you half as much as practical tasks, no matter how complex these might be. If you were to find yourself cast up on a desert island you would have all the necessities of life sorted out in a flash. This is not to suggest that you always recognise this potential in yourself. The problem here is that a very definite lack of self-belief is inclined to make you think that almost anyone else in the world has the edge when it comes to talent.

Another of your greatest resources is your creative potential. You always have the knack of knowing what looks and feels just right. This is as true when it comes to decorating your home as it is regarding matters out there in the big, wide world. If this skill could be allied to confidence on a regular basis, there would be little or nothing to stop you. You may well possess specific skills which others definitely don't have, and you get on best when these are really needed.

Taureans don't mind dealing with routine matters and you have a good administrative ability in a number of different fields. With a deeply intuitive streak (when you are willing to recognise it), it isn't usually hard for you to work out how any particular individual would react under given circumstances. Where you fall down on occasions is that you don't always recognise the great advantages that are yours for the taking, and self-belief could hardly be considered the Taurean's greatest virtue.

Taurus people are good at making lists, even if these are of the mental variety. Your natural warmth makes it possible for you to find friends where others would not, and the sort of advice that you offer is considered and sensible. People feel they can rely on you, a fact that could prove to be one of the most important of your resources. There is nothing at all wrong with using this ability to feather your own nest, particularly since you are not the sort of person who would willingly stand on those around you in order to get where you want to go.

Beneath the surface

To say that you are deep would be a definite understatement. Only you know how far down into the basement some of your considerations and emotions actually go. Because you exhibit a generally practical face to the world at large the true scope of the Taurean mind remains something of a mystery to those around you. Certainly you seem to be uncomplicated and even a little superficial at times, though nothing could be further from the truth. Very little happens to you that fails to be filed away in some recess or other of that great interior that is your mind's library. It may be because of this that Taurus is well known for being able to bear a grudge for a long time. However, what is sometimes forgotten is that you never let a kindness from someone else go without reward, even though it may take you a very long time to find a way to say thank you.

Affairs of the heart are of special importance to you and ties of the romantic kind go as deep as any emotion. Once you love you tend to do so quite unconditionally. It takes months or years of upsets to shake your faith in love, and it's a fact that even in these days of marital splits, Taureans are far more likely than most signs of the zodiac to remain hitched. The simple fact is that you believe in loyalty, absolutely and irrevocably. The thought of letting anyone down once you have given your word is almost unthinkable and if such a situation does occur there are almost always quite definite mitigating factors.

Rules and regulations are easy for you to deal with because you have a natural tendency to order. You are also fairly good at dealing with routines and probably have your own life well sorted out as a result. A word of caution is necessary only when this internal need for order extends too much into your external life. Taureans can be fanatical about having a tidy house or for making things work out exactly as they would wish in a work sense. These tendencies start within the recesses of your own, often closed, mind. The way forward here is to throw open the doors and windows now and again and to let those around you know how you function internally. It isn't easy, because you are quite a closed book at heart. However the exercise is well worthwhile and the results can be quite breathtaking.

Making the best of yourself

Anyone who wants to work to the best of their ability first needs a good deal of self-knowledge. In your case this means recognising just what you are capable of doing and then concentrating in these directions. Of course it's only human nature to be all the things we are not, but this tendency runs deeper in you than it does in the majority of individuals. Use your natural kindness to the full and ally this to your practical ability to get things done. Sorting things out is easy for you, so easy in fact that you sometimes fail to realise that not everyone has these skills to the same extent.

Confidence definitely seems to be evident in the way you deal with the world at large. Of course you know that this often isn't the case, but that doesn't matter. It's the way the world at large views you that counts, so keep moving forward, even on those occasions when you are shaking inside. Use your naturally creative skills to the full and cultivate that innate sense of order in ways that benefit you and the world at a very practical level.

Avoid the tendency to be stubborn by convincing yourself that so many things 'simply don't matter'. An inability to move, simply because you feel annoyed or aggrieved, is certainly going to be more of a hindrance than a help – though there are occasions when, like all facets of nature, it's essential. Cultivate the more cheerful qualities that are endemic to your nature and be prepared to mix freely with as many different sorts of people as you possibly can. Be willing to take on new responsibilities because the more you are able to do so, the greater is your natural sense of self-worth. Stitching all these qualities together and using them to your own advantage isn't always easy, but pays handsomely in the end.

The impressions you give

This is a very interesting section as far as the sign of Taurus is concerned. The reason is very simply that you fail on so many occasions to betray the sheer depth of your own Earth-sign nature. That doesn't mean to say that you come across badly to others. On the contrary, you are probably a very popular person, except with those people who mistreat or cheat others. You have a great sense of what is right, and don't tend to deviate from a point of view once you've come to terms with it.

The world sees you as capable, cheerful and generally active, though with a tendency to be sluggish and lethargic on occasions. Perhaps Taurus needs to explain itself more because even when you are not at your most vibrant best there are invariably reasons. You can be quite secretive, though only usually about yourself. This can make life with the Taurean something of a guessing game on occasions. Certainly you appear to be much more fixed in your attitude than might often be the case. Why should this be so? It's mainly because you do have extremely definite ideas about specific matters, and since you sometimes display these it's natural that others pigeon-hole you as a very 'definite' sort. Actually this is far from being the whole truth but, once again, if you don't explain yourself, others can be left in the dark.

You almost certainly are not short of friends. People recognise that you are friendly, tolerant and extremely supportive. You give the impression of being very trustworthy and people know that they can rely on you to act in a specific manner. If this appears to make you somewhat predictable it doesn't really matter because you are deeply loved, and that's what counts. One fact is almost certain – the world has a greater regard for you in a general sense than you have for yourself.

The way forward

The ideal life for the Taurus subject seems to be one that is settled and happy, with not too much upheaval and plenty of order. Whether or not this truly turns out to be the case depends on a number of factors. For starters, even those born under the sign of the Bull have a boredom threshold. This means that having to respond to change and diversity probably does you more good than you might at first think. At the same time you won't know exactly what you are capable of doing unless you really stretch yourself, and that's something that you are not always willing to do.

You do function best from within loving relationships, and although you can be very passionate, once you have given your heart you don't tend to change your mind readily. Personal and domestic contentment are worth a great deal to you because they represent the platform upon which you build the rest of your life. You don't make a good itinerant and probably won't indulge in travel for its own sake. Of course it does you good to get around, since anything that broadens your horizons has got to be an advantage, but you'll probably always maintain a solid home base and relish the prospect of coming back to it as frequently as possible.

Most Taureans are family people. You can be a capable parent, though tend to be a little more authoritarian than some types. Keeping an ordered sort of life is at the base of your psychology, so that even when you are young and less tidy-minded there is always a basic desire for self-discipline. This often extends to your work, where you are extremely capable and can quite easily work under your own supervision. You recognise the beautiful in all spheres of life and tend to gravitate towards clean and sanitary surroundings.

In matters of health you tend to be fairly robust, though you can suffer somewhat with headaches, often brought about as a result of a stiff neck and stress. This latter is what you should avoid as much as possible. Saying what you feel, and listening carefully to the responses, is definitely of great importance. The more you learn, the wiser you become. This makes you the natural resort of others when they need help and advice. If you try not to underestimate your own abilities, you can rise as far in life as the world at large thinks you are capable of doing. At the end of the day it is important to recognise your popularity. In all probability your friends have a much higher opinion of you than the one you cultivate for yourself.

TAURUS ON THE CUSP

Astrological profiles are altered for those people born at either the beginning or the end of a zodiac sign, or, more properly, on the cusps of a sign. In the case of Taurus this would be on the 21st of April and for two or three days after, and similarly at the end of the sign, probably from the 18th to the 21st of May.

The Aries Cusp – April 21st to April 24th

Although you have all the refinement, breeding and creative flair of the true Taurean, you are definitely more of a go-getter. Knowing what you want from life there is a slight possibility that you might be accused of being bossy and sometimes this slightly hurts your Taurean sensitivity. You have plenty of energy to get through the things that you see as being important but it is quite possible that those around you don't always see things in the same light, and this can be annoying to you. Like the typical Taurean you have great reserves of energy and can work long and hard towards any particular objective although, because Aries is also in attendance, you may push yourself slightly harder than is strictly necessary. Your temper is variable and you may not always display the typical Taurean patience with those around you.

It is possible for Taurus to 'wait in the wings' deliberately and therefore to lose out on some of the most important potential gains as a result. In your case, this is much less likely. You don't worry too much about speaking your mind. You are loving and kind, but even family members know that they will only be able to push you so far. At work, you are capable and have executive ability. Like the Taurean you don't really care for getting your hands dirty, but if needs must you can pitch in with the best of them and enjoy a challenge. You don't worry as much as some of your Taurean friends do, but all the same you regularly expect too much of your nervous system and need frequent periods of rest.

Try not to impose your will on those around you and be content to allow things to happen on their own sometimes. This might not be an easy thing for the Aries-cusp Taurean but it's one of the sure ways to success. Confidence isn't lacking and neither is basic patience, but they do have to be encouraged and nurtured.

The Gemini Cusp – May 18th to May 21st

Oh, what a happy person you are – and how much the world loves you for it! This is definitely the more potentially fortunate of the two Taurean cusps, or at least that is how the majority of the people who know you would view it. The fact is that you are bright and breezy, easygoing and sometimes fickle on occasions, but supporting these trends is a patient, generally contented attitude to life that is both refreshing and inspiring. Getting others on your side is not hard and you have plenty of energy when it is needed the most. All the same you are quite capable of dozing in the sun occasionally and probably put far less stress on your nervous system than either Taurus or Gemini when taken alone.

You don't care too much for routines and you love variety, but yet you retain the creative and artistic qualities that come with the sign of the Bull. You work well and with confidence, but would be very likely to change direction in your career at some stage in your life and are not half so tied to routine as is usually the case for Taurus. With a friendly, and even a passionate, approach to matters of the heart you are an attentive lover and a fond parent. Most people know what you really are because you are only too willing to show them. Working out the true motivations that lurk within your soul is part of your personal search to know 'self' and is extremely important.

All in all, you have exactly what it takes to get on in life and a sense of joy and fun that makes you good to know. Patience balances your need to 'get going', whilst your mischievous streak lightens the load of the sign of Taurus which can, on occasions, take itself rather more seriously than it should.

There are many ways of coping with the requirements of life and, at one time or another, it is likely that you will try them all out. But above and beyond your need to experiment you know what is most important to you and that will always be your ultimate goal. What matters the most is your smile, which is enduring and ever alluring.

TAURUS AND ITS ASCENDANTS

The nature of every individual on the planet is composed of the rich variety of zodiac signs and planetary positions that were present at the time of their birth. Your Sun sign, which in your case is Taurus, is one of the many factors when it comes to assessing the unique person you are. Probably the most important consideration, other than your Sun sign, is to establish the zodiac sign that was rising over the eastern horizon at the time that you were born. This is your Ascending or Rising sign. Most popular astrology fails to take account of the Ascendant, and yet its importance remains with you from the very moment of your birth, through every day of your life. The Ascendant is evident in the way you approach the world, and so, when meeting a person for the first time, it is this astrological influence that you are most likely to notice first. Our Ascending sign essentially represents what we appear to be, while the Sun sign is what we feel inside ourselves.

The Ascendant also has the potential for modifying our overall nature. For example, if you were born at a time of day when Taurus was passing over the eastern horizon (this would be around the time of dawn) then you would be classed as a double Taurus. As such, you would typify this zodiac sign, both internally and in your dealings with others. However, if your Ascendant sign turned out to be a Fire sign, such as Leo, there would be a profound alteration of nature, away from the expected qualities of Taurus.

One of the reasons why popular astrology often ignores the Ascendant is that it has always been rather difficult to establish. We have found a way to make this possible by devising an easy-to-use table, which you will find on page 157 of this book. Using this, you can establish your Ascendant sign at a glance. You will need to know your rough time of birth, then it is simply a case of following the instructions.

For those readers who have no idea of their time of birth it might be worth allowing a good friend, or perhaps your partner, to read through the section that follows this introduction. Someone who deals with you on a regular basis may easily discover your Ascending sign, even though you could have some difficulty establishing it for yourself. A good understanding of this component of your nature is essential if you want to be aware of that 'other person' who is responsible for the way you make contact with the world at large. Your Sun sign, Ascendant sign, and the other pointers in this book will, together, allow you a far better understanding of what makes you tick as an individual. Peeling back the different layers of your astrological make-up can be an enlightening experience, and the Ascendant may represent one of the most important layers of all.

Taurus with Taurus Ascendant

The world would see you as being fairly typical of the sign of Taurus, so you are careful, sensitive, well bred and, if other astrological trends agree, very creative. Nothing pleases you more than a tidy environment to live in and a peaceful life. You probably believe that there is a place for everything and will do your best to keep it all where it should be. It's a pity that this sometimes includes people, and you are certain to get rather irritated if they don't behave in the way that you would expect. Despite this, you are generally understanding and are very capable of giving and receiving affection.

Not everyone knows the real you, however, and it is sometimes difficult to tell the world those most personal details that can be locked deep inside. At an emotional level you tend to idealise love somewhat, though if anything this presents itself to the world as a slight 'coldness' on occasions. This is far from the truth, but your tidy mind demands that even the most intimate processes are subjected to the same sense of order with which you view the world at large. Unlike many sign combinations, you don't really rely on the help and support of others because you are more than capable yourself. In the main you live a happy life and have the ability to pass on this trait to those you care for.

Taurus with Gemini Ascendant

This is a generally happy combination which finds you better able to externalise the cultured and creative qualities which are inherent in your Taurean nature. You love to be around interesting and stimulating people and tend to be much more talkative than the typical Taurean is expected to be. The reason why Gemini helps here is because it lightens the load somewhat. Taurus is not the most introspective sign of the zodiac, but it does have that quality, and a good dose of Gemini allows you to speak your mind more freely and, as a result, to know yourself better too.

Although your mind tends to be fairly logical, you also enjoy flashes of insight that can cause you to behave in a less rational way from time to time. This is probably no bad thing because life will never be boring with you around. You try to convince yourself that you take on board all the many and varied opinions that come back at you from others, though there is a slight danger of intellectual snobbery if the responses you get are not the expected ones. You particularly like clean houses, funny people and probably fast cars. Financial rewards can come thick and fast to the Gemini-Ascendant Taurean when the logical but inspirational mind is harnessed to practical matters.

Taurus with Cancer Ascendant

Your main aim in life seems to be to look after everyone and everything that you come across. From your deepest and most enduring human love, right down to the birds in the park, you really do care and you show that natural affection in a thousand different ways. Your nature is sensitive and you are easily moved to tears, though this does not prevent you from pitching in and doing practical things to assist at just about any level. There is a danger that you could stifle those same people whom you set out to assist, and people with this zodiac combination are often unwilling, or unable, to allow their children to grow and leave the nest. More time spent considering what suits you would be no bad thing, but the problem is that you find it almost impossible to imagine any situation that doesn't involve your most basic need, which is to nurture.

You appear not to possess a selfish streak, though it sometimes turns out that, in being certain that you understand the needs and wants of the world, you are nevertheless treading on their toes. This eventual realisation can be very painful, but it isn't a stick with which you should beat yourself because at heart you are one of the kindest people imaginable. Your sense of fair play means that you are a quiet social reformer at heart.

Taurus with Leo Ascendant

Oh dear, this can be rather a hedonistic combination. The trouble is that Taurus tends to have a great sense of what looks and feels right, whilst Leo, being a Cat, is inclined to preen itself on almost any occasion. The combination tends towards self-love, which is all too likely for someone who is perfect. But don't be too dispirited about these facts because there is a great deal going for you in other ways. For a start you have one of the warmest hearts to be found anywhere and you are so brave that others marvel at the courage you display. The mountains that you climb may not be of the large, rocky sort, but you manage to find plenty of pinnacles to scale all the same, and you invariably get to the top.

Routines might bore you a little more than would be the case with Taurus alone, but you don't mind being alone. Why should you? You are probably the nicest person you know! Thus if you were ever to be cast up on a deserted island you would people the place all on your own, and there would never be any crime, untidiness or arguments. Problems only arise when other people are involved. However, in social settings you are charming, good to know and full of ideas that really have legs. You preserve your youth well into middle age, but at base you can tend to worry more than is good for you.

Taurus with Virgo Ascendant

This combination tends to amplify the Taurean qualities that you naturally possess and this is the case because both Taurus and Virgo are Earth signs. However, there are certain factors related to Virgo that show themselves very differently than the sign's cousin Taurus. Virgo is more fussy, nervy and and pedantic than Taurus and all of these qualities are going to show up in your nature at one level or another. On the plus side, you might be slightly less concerned about having a perfect home and a perfect family, and your interest in life appears at a more direct level than that of the true Taurean. You care very much about your home and family and are very loyal to your friends. It's true that you sometimes tend to try and take them over, and you can also show a marked tendency to dominate, but your heart is in the right place, and most people recognise that your caring is genuine.

One problem is that there are very few shades of grey in your life, which is certainly not the case for other zodiac sign combinations. Living your life in the way that you do, there isn't much room for compromise, and this fact alone can prove to be something of a problem where relationships are concerned. In a personal sense you need a partner who is willing to be organised and one who relies heavily on your judgements, which don't change very often.

Taurus with Libra Ascendant

A fortunate combination in many ways, this is a double Venus rulership, since both Taurus and Libra are heavily reliant on the planet of love. You are social, amiable and a natural diplomat, anxious to please and ready to care for just about anyone who shows interest in you. You hate disorder, which means that there is a place for everything and everything in its place. This can throw up the odd paradox, however, since being half Libran you cannot always work out where that place ought to be! You deal with life in a humorous way and are quite capable of seeing the absurd in yourself, as well as in others. Your heart is no bigger than that of the dyed-in-the-wool Taurean, but it sits rather closer to the surface and so others recognise it more.

On those occasions when you know you are standing on firm ground you can show great confidence, even if you have to be ready to change some of your opinions at the drop of a hat. When this happens you can be quite at odds with yourself, because Taurus doesn't take very many U-turns, whereas Libra does. Don't expect to know yourself too well, and keep looking for the funny side of things, because it is within humour that you forge the sort of life that suits you best.

Taurus with Scorpio Ascendant

The first, last and most important piece of advice for you is not to take yourself, or anyone else, too seriously. This might be rather a tall order because Scorpio intensifies the deeper qualities of Taurus and can make you rather lacking in the sense of humour that we all need to live our lives in this most imperfect of worlds. You are naturally sensuous by nature. This shows itself in a host of ways. In all probability you can spend hours in the bath, love to treat yourself to good food and drink and take your greatest pleasure in neat and orderly surroundings. On occasions this can alienate you from those who live in the same house, because other people do need to use the bathroom from time to time, and they cannot remain tidy indefinitely.

You tend to worry a great deal about things which are really not very important, but don't take this statement too seriously or you will begin to worry about this, too! You often need to lighten up and should always do your best to tell yourself that most things are not half so important as they seem to be. Be careful over the selection of a life partner and if possible choose someone who is naturally funny and who does not take life anywhere near as seriously as you are inclined to do. At work you are more than capable and in all probability everyone relies heavily on your wise judgements.

Taurus with Sagittarius Ascendant

A dual nature is evident here, and if it doesn't serve to confuse you, it will certainly be a cause of concern to many of the people with whom you share your life. You like to have a good time and are a natural party-goer. On such occasions you are accommodating, chatty and good to know. But contrast this with the quieter side of Taurus, which is directly opposed to your Sagittarian qualities. The opposition of forces is easy for you to deal with because you inhabit your own body and mind all the time, but it's far less easy for friends and relatives to understand. So on those occasions when you decide that, socially speaking, enough is enough, you may have trouble explaining this to the twelve people who are waiting outside your door with party hats and whoopee cushions.

Confidence to do almost anything is not far from the forefront of your mind and you readily embark on adventures that would have some types flapping about in horror. Here again, it is important to realise that we are not all built the same way and that gentle coaxing is sometimes necessary to bring others round to your point of view. If you really have a fault it could be that you are so busy being your own, rather less than predictable self, that you fail to take the rest of the world into account.

Taurus with Capricorn Ascendant

It might appear on the surface that you are not the most interesting person in the world. This is a pity, for you have an active though very logical mind, so logical in some instances that you would have a great deal in common with Mr Spock. This is the thorn in your flesh, or rather the flesh of everyone else, since you are probably quite happy being exactly what you are. You can think things through in a clear and very practical way and end up taking decisions that are balanced, eminently sensible, but, on occasions, rather dull.

Actually there is a fun machine somewhere deep within that Earth-sign nature and those who know you the best will recognise the fact. Often this combination is attended by a deep and biting sense of humour, but it's of the sort that less intelligent and considered types would find rather difficult to recognise. It is likely that you have no lack of confidence in your own judgement and you have all the attributes necessary to do very well on the financial front. Slow and steady progress is your way and you need to be quite certain before you commit yourself to any new venture. This is a zodiac combination that can soak up years of stress and numerous difficulties, yet still come out on top. Nothing holds you back for long and you tend to be very brave.

Taurus with Aquarius Ascendant

There is nothing that you fail to think about deeply and with great intensity. You are wise, honest and very scientific in your approach to life. Routines are necessary in life, but you have most of them sorted out well in advance and so always have time to look at the next interesting fact. If you don't spend all your time watching documentaries on the television set, you make a good friend and love to socialise. Most of the great discoveries of the world were probably made by people with this sort of astrological combination, though your nature is rather 'odd' on occasions and so can be rather difficult for others to understand.

You may be most surprised when others tell you that you are eccentric, but you don't really mind too much because for half of the time you are not inhabiting the same world as the rest of us. Because you can be delightfully dotty you are probably much loved and cherished by your friends, of which there are likely to be many. Family members probably adore you too and you can be guaranteed to entertain anyone with whom you come into contact. The only fly in the ointment is that you sometimes lose track of reality, whatever that might be, and fly high in your own atmosphere of rarefied possibilities.

Taurus with Pisces Ascendant

You are clearly a very sensitive type of person and that sometimes makes it rather difficult for others to know how they might best approach you. Private and deep, you are nevertheless socially inclined on many occasions. However, because your nature is bottomless it is possible that some types would actually accuse you of being shallow. How can this come about? Well, it's simple really. The fact is that you rarely show anyone what is going on in the deepest recesses of your mind and so your responses can appear to be trite or even ill-considered. This is far from the truth, as those who are allowed into the 'inner sanctum' would readily admit. You are something of a sensualist, and relish staying in bed late and simply pleasing yourself for days on end. However, you are a Taurean at heart so you desire a tidy environment in which to live your usually long life.

You are able to deal with the routine aspects of life quite well and can be a capable worker once you are up and firing on all cylinders. It is very important that you maintain an interest in what you are doing because the recesses of your dreamy mind can sometimes appear to be infinitely more attractive. Your imagination is second to none and this fact can often be turned to your advantage.

Taurus with Aries Ascendant

This is a steady combination, so much so that even experienced astrologers would be unlikely to recognise that the Aries quality is present at all, unless of course they came to know you very well. Your approach to life tends to be slow and considered and there is a great danger that you could suppress those feelings that others of your kind would be only too willing to verbalise. To compensate, you are deeply creative and will think matters through much more readily than more dominant Aries types would be inclined to do. In your dealings with the world, you are, nevertheless, somewhat locked inside yourself and can struggle to achieve the level of communication that you so desperately need. Frustration might follow, were it not for the fact that you possess a quiet determination that, to those in the know, is the clearest window through to your Taurean soul.

The care for others is strong and you certainly demonstrate this at all levels. The fact is that you live a great percentage of your life in service to the people you take to, whilst at the same time being able to shut the door firmly in the face of people who irritate or anger you. You are deeply motivated towards family relationships.

THE MOON AND THE PART IT PLAYS IN YOUR LIFE

In astrology the Moon is probably the single most important heavenly body after the Sun. Its unique position, as partner to the Earth on its journey around the solar system, means that the Moon appears to pass through the signs of the zodiac extremely quickly. The zodiac position of the Moon at the time of your birth plays a great part in personal character and is especially significant in the build-up of your emotional nature.

Your Own Moon Sign

Discovering the position of the Moon at the time of your birth has always been notoriously difficult because tracking the complex zodiac positions of the Moon is not easy. This process has been reduced to three simple stages with our Lunar Tables. A breakdown of the Moon's zodiac positions can be found from page 35 onwards, so that once you know what your Moon Sign is, you can see what part this plays in the overall build-up of your personal character.

If you follow the instructions on the next page you will soon be able to work out exactly what zodiac sign the Moon occupied on the day that you were born and you can then go on to compare the reading for this position with those of your Sun sign and your Ascendant. It is partly the comparison between these three important positions that goes towards making you the unique individual you are.

HOW TO DISCOVER YOUR MOON SIGN

This is a three-stage process. You may need a pen and a piece of paper but if you follow the instructions below the process should only take a minute or so.

STAGE 1 First of all you need to know the Moon Age at the time of your birth. If you look at Moon Table 1, on page 33, you will find all the years between 1910 and 2008 down the left side. Find the year of your birth and then trace across to the right to the month of your birth. Where the two intersect you will find a number. This is the date of the New Moon in the month that you were born. You now need to count forward the number of days between the New Moon and your own birthday. For example, if the New Moon in the month of your birth was shown as being the 6th and you were born on the 20th, your Moon Age Day would be 14. If the New Moon in the month of your birth came after your birthday, you need to count forward from the New Moon in the previous month. If you were born in a Leap Year, remember to count the 29th February. You can tell if your birth year was a Leap Year if the last two digits can be divided by four. Whatever the result, jot this number down so that you do not forget it.

STAGE 2 Take a look at Moon Table 2 on page 34. Down the left hand column look for the date of your birth. Now trace across to the month of your birth. Where the two meet you will find a letter. Copy this letter down alongside your Moon Age Day.

STAGE 3 Moon Table 3 on page 34 will supply you with the zodiac sign the Moon occupied on the day of your birth. Look for your Moon Age Day down the left hand column and then for the letter you found in Stage 2. Where the two converge you will find a zodiac sign and this is the sign occupied by the Moon on the day that you were born.

Your Zodiac Moon Sign Explained

You will find a profile of all zodiac Moon Signs on pages 35 to 38, showing in yet another way how astrology helps to make you into the individual that you are. In each daily entry of the Astral Diary you can find the zodiac position of the Moon for every day of the year. This also allows you to discover your lunar birthdays. Since the Moon passes through all the signs of the zodiac in about a month, you can expect something like twelve lunar birthdays each year. At these times you are likely to be emotionally steady and able to make the sort of decisions that have real, lasting value.

MOON TABLE 1

YEAR	MAR	APR	MAY	YEAR	MAR	APR	MAY	YEAR	MAR	APR	MAY
1910	11	9	9	1943	6	4	4	1976	30	29	29
1911	30	28	28	1944	24	22	22	1977	19	18	18
1912	19	18	17	1945	14	12	11	1978	9	7	7
1913	7	6	5	1946	3	2	1/30	1979	27	26	26
1914	26	24	24	1947	21	20	19	1980	16	15	14
1915	15	13	13	1948	11	9	9	1981	6	4	4
1916	5	3	2	1949	29	28	27	1982	24	23	21
1917	23	22	20	1950	18	17	17	1983	14	13	12
1918	12	11	10	1951	7	6	6	1984	2	1	1/30
1919	2/31	30	29	1952	25	24	23	1985	21	20	19
1920	20	18	18	1953	15	13	13	1986	10	9	8
1921	9	8	7	1954	5	3	2	1987	29	28	27
1922	28	27	26	1955	24	22	21	1988	18	16	15
1923	17	16	15	1956	12	11	10	1989	7	6	5
1924	5	4	3	1957	1/31	29	29	1990	26	25	24
1925	24	23	22	1958	20	19	18	1991	15	13	13
1926	14	12	11	1959	9	8	7	1992	4	3	2
1927	3	2	1/30	1960	27	26	26	1993	24	22	21
1928	21	20	19	1961	16	15	14	1994	12	11	10
1929	11	9	9	1962	6	5	4	1995	30	29	29
1930	30	28	28	1963	25	23	23	1996	19	18	18
1931	19	18	17	1964	14	12	11	1997	9	7	6
1932	7	6	5	1965	2	1	1/30	1998	27	26	25
1933	26	24	24	1966	21	20	19	1999	17	16	15
1934	15	13	13	1967	10	9	8	2000	6	4	4
1935	5	3	2	1968	29	28	27	2001	24	23	22
1936	23	21	20	1969	18	16	15	2002	13	12	10
1937	13	12	10	1970	7	6	6	2003	2	1	1/30
1938	2/31	30	29	1971	26	25	24	2004	21	19	18
1939	20	19	19	1972	15	13	13	2005	10	8	8
1940	9	7	7	1973	5	3	2	2006	29	27	27
1941	27	26	26	1974	24	22	21	2007	18	17	15
1942	16	15	15	1975	12	11	11	2008	7	6	5

33

TABLE 2

MOON TABLE 3

DAY	APR	MAY	M/D	J	K	L	M	N	O	P
1	J	M	0	AR	TA	TA	TA	GE	GE	GE
2	J	M	1	TA	TA	TA	GE	GE	GE	CA
3	J	M	2	TA	TA	GE	GE	GE	CA	CA
4	J	M	3	TA	GE	GE	GE	CA	CA	CA
5	J	M	4	GE	GE	GE	CA	CA	CA	LE
6	J	M	5	GE	CA	CA	CA	LE	LE	LE
7	J	M	6	CA	CA	CA	LE	LE	LE	VI
8	J	M	7	CA	CA	LE	LE	LE	VI	VI
9	J	M	8	CA	LE	LE	LE	VI	VI	VI
10	J	M	9	LE	LE	VI	VI	VI	LI	LI
11	K	M	10	LE	VI	VI	VI	LI	LI	LI
12	K	N	11	VI	VI	VI	LI	LI	SC	SC
13	K	N	12	VI	VI	LI	LI	LI	SC	SC
14	K	N	13	VI	LI	LI	LI	SC	SC	SC
15	K	N	14	LI	LI	LI	SC	SC	SA	SA
16	K	N	15	LI	SC	SC	SC	SA	SA	SA
17	K	N	16	SC	SC	SC	SA	SA	SA	CP
18	K	N	17	SC	SC	SA	SA	SA	CP	CP
19	K	N	18	SC	SA	SA	SA	CP	CP	CP
20	K	N	19	SA	SA	SA	CP	CP	CP	AQ
21	L	N	20	SA	CP	CP	CP	AQ	AQ	AQ
22	L	O	21	CP	CP	CP	AQ	AQ	AQ	PI
23	L	O	22	CP	CP	AQ	AQ	AQ	PI	PI
24	L	O	23	CP	AQ	AQ	AQ	PI	PI	PI
25	L	O	24	AQ	AQ	AQ	PI	PI	PI	AR
26	L	O	25	AQ	PI	PI	PI	AR	AR	AR
27	L	O	26	PI	PI	PI	AR	AR	AR	TA
28	L	O	27	PI	PI	AR	AR	AR	TA	TA
29	L	O	28	PI	AR	AR	AR	TA	TA	TA
30	L	O	29	AR	AR	AR	TA	TA	TA	GE
31	–	O								

AR = Aries, TA = Taurus, GE = Gemini, CA = Cancer, LE = Leo, VI = Virgo
LI = Libra, SC = Scorpio, SA = Sagittarius, CP = Capricorn, AQ = Aquarius, PI = Pisces

MOON SIGNS

Moon in Aries

You have a strong imagination, courage, determination and a desire to do things in your own way and forge your own path through life.

Originality is a key attribute; you are seldom stuck for ideas although your mind is changeable and you could take the time to focus on individual tasks. Often quick-tempered, you take orders from few people and live life at a fast pace. Avoid health problems by taking regular time out for rest and relaxation.

Emotionally, it is important that you talk to those you are closest to and work out your true feelings. Once you discover that people are there to help, there is less necessity for you to do everything yourself.

Moon in Taurus

The Moon in Taurus gives you a courteous and friendly manner, which means you are likely to have many friends.

The good things in life mean a lot to you, as Taurus is an Earth sign that delights in experiences which please the senses. Hence you are probably a lover of good food and drink, which may in turn mean you need to keep an eye on the bathroom scales, especially as looking good is also important to you.

Emotionally you are fairly stable and you stick by your own standards. Taureans do not respond well to change. Intuition also plays an important part in your life.

Moon in Gemini

You have a warm-hearted character, sympathetic and eager to help others. At times reserved, you can also be articulate and chatty: this is part of the paradox of Gemini, which always brings duplicity to the nature. You are interested in current affairs, have a good intellect, and are good company and likely to have many friends. Most of your friends have a high opinion of you and would be ready to defend you should the need arise. However, this is usually unnecessary, as you are quite capable of defending yourself in any verbal confrontation.

Travel is important to your inquisitive mind and you find intellectual stimulus in mixing with people from different cultures. You also gain much from reading, writing and the arts but you do need plenty of rest and relaxation in order to avoid fatigue.

Moon in Cancer

The Moon in Cancer at the time of birth is a fortunate position as Cancer is the Moon's natural home. This means that the qualities of compassion and understanding given by the Moon are especially enhanced in your nature, and you are friendly and sociable and cope well with emotional pressures. You cherish home and family life, and happily do the domestic tasks. Your surroundings are important to you and you hate squalor and filth. You are likely to have a love of music and poetry.

Your basic character, although at times changeable like the Moon itself, depends on symmetry. You aim to make your surroundings comfortable and harmonious, for yourself and those close to you.

Moon in Leo

The best qualities of the Moon and Leo come together to make you warm-hearted, fair, ambitious and self-confident. With good organisational abilities, you invariably rise to a position of responsibility in your chosen career. This is fortunate as you don't enjoy being an 'also-ran' and would rather be an important part of a small organisation than a menial in a large one.

You should be lucky in love, and happy, provided you put in the effort to make a comfortable home for yourself and those close to you. It is likely that you will have a love of pleasure, sport, music and literature. Life brings you many rewards, most of them as a direct result of your own efforts, although you may be luckier than average and ready to make the best of any situation.

Moon in Virgo

You are endowed with good mental abilities and a keen receptive memory, but you are never ostentatious or pretentious. Naturally quite reserved, you still have many friends, especially of the opposite sex. Marital relationships must be discussed carefully and worked at so that they remain harmonious, as personal attachments can be a problem if you do not give them your full attention.

Talented and persevering, you possess artistic qualities and are a good homemaker. Earning your honours through genuine merit, you work long and hard towards your objectives but show little pride in your achievements. Many short journeys will be undertaken in your life.

Moon in Libra

With the Moon in Libra you are naturally popular and make friends easily. People like you, probably more than you realise, you bring fun to a party and are a natural diplomat. For all its good points, Libra is not the most stable of astrological signs and, as a result, your emotions can be a little unstable too. Therefore, although the Moon in Libra is said to be good for love and marriage, your Sun sign and Rising sign will have an important effect on your emotional and loving qualities.

You must remember to relate to others in your decision-making. Co-operation is crucial because Libra represents the 'balance' of life that can only be achieved through harmonious relationships. Conformity is not easy for you because Libra, an Air sign, likes its independence.

Moon in Scorpio

Some people might call you pushy. In fact, all you really want to do is to live life to the full and protect yourself and your family from the pressures of life. Take care to avoid giving the impression of being sarcastic or impulsive and use your energies wisely and constructively.

You have great courage and you invariably achieve your goals by force of personality and sheer effort. You are fond of mystery and are good at predicting the outcome of situations and events. Travel experiences can be beneficial to you.

You may experience problems if you do not take time to examine your motives in a relationship, and also if you allow jealousy, always a feature of Scorpio, to cloud your judgement.

Moon in Sagittarius

The Moon in Sagittarius helps to make you a generous individual with humanitarian qualities and a kind heart. Restlessness may be intrinsic as your mind is seldom still. Perhaps because of this, you have a need for change that could lead you to several major moves during your adult life. You are not afraid to stand your ground when you know your judgement is right, you speak directly and have good intuition.

At work you are quick, efficient and versatile and so you make an ideal employee. You need work to be intellectually demanding and do not enjoy tedious routines.

In relationships, you anger quickly if faced with stupidity or deception, though you are just as quick to forgive and forget. Emotionally, there are times when your heart rules your head.

Moon in Capricorn

The Moon in Capricorn makes you popular and likely to come into the public eye in some way. The watery Moon is not entirely comfortable in the Earth sign of Capricorn and this may lead to some difficulties in the early years of life. An initial lack of creative ability and indecision must be overcome before the true qualities of patience and perseverance inherent in Capricorn can show through.

You have good administrative ability and are a capable worker and if you are careful you can accumulate wealth. But you must be cautious and take professional advice in partnerships, as you are open to deception. You may be interested in social or welfare work which suit your organisational skills and sympathy for others.

Moon in Aquarius

The Moon in Aquarius makes you an active and agreeable person with a friendly, easy-going nature. Sympathetic to the needs of others, you flourish in a laid-back atmosphere. You are broad minded, fair and open to suggestion, although sometimes you have an unconventional quality which others can find hard to understand.

You are interested in the strange and curious, and in old article and places. You enjoy trips to these places and gain much from them. Political, scientific and educational work interests you and you might choose a career in science or technology.

Money-wise, you make gains through innovation and concentration and Lunar Aquarians often tackle more than one job at a time. In love you are kind and honest.

Moon in Pisces

You have a kind, sympathetic nature, somewhat retiring at times, but you always take account of others' feelings and help when you can.

Personal relationships may be problematic, but as life goes on you can learn from your experiences and develop a better understanding of yourself and the world around you.

You have a fondness for travel, appreciate beauty and harmony and hate disorder and strife. You may be fond of literature and would make a good writer or speaker yourself. You have a creative imagination and may come across as an incurable romantic. You have strong intuition, maybe bordering on a mediumistic quality which sets you apart from the mass. You may not be rich in cash terms, but your personal gifts are worth more than gold.

TAURUS IN LOVE

Discover how compatible you are with people from the same and other signs of the zodiac. Five stars equals a match made in heaven!

Taurus meets Taurus

A certainty for complete success or absolute failure. Taurus has enough self-knowledge to recognise the strengths of a fellow Taurean, so these two can live in harmony. Both will be tidy and live in comfortable surroundings. Two Taureans seldom argue and will be good friends. But something may be lacking – a spark that doesn't ignite. Passion is important and Taurus reflects, rather than creates it. The prognosis is good, but someone must turn the heat up to get things really cooking. Star rating: ****

Taurus meets Gemini

Gemini people can infuriate the generally steady Taurean nature as they are so untidy, which is a complete reversal of the Taurean ethos. At first this won't matter; Mr or Miss Gemini is enchanting, entertaining and very different. But time will tell, and that's why this potential relationship only has two stars. There is hope, however, because Taurus can curb some of the excesses of the Twins, whilst Gemini is capable of preventing the Bull from taking itself too seriously. Star rating: **

Taurus meets Cancer

This pair will have the tidiest house in the street – every stick of furniture in place, and no errant blade of grass daring to spoil the lawn. But things inside the relationship might not be quite so ship-shape as both signs need, but don't offer, encouragement. There's plenty of affection, but few incentives for mutual progress. This might not prevent material success, but an enduring relationship isn't based on money alone. Passion is essential, and both parties need to realise and aim for that. Star rating: **

Taurus meets Leo

Here we find a generally successful pairing, which frequently leads to an enduring relationship. Taurus needs stimulation which Leo is happy to offer, while Leo responds well to the Bull's sense of order. The essence of the relationship is balance, but it may be achieved with wild swings of the scales on the way, so don't expect a quiet life, though this pair will enjoy a reconciliation after an argument! Material success is probable and, as both like children, a family is likely. Star rating: ***

Taurus meets Virgo

This is a difficult basis for a successful relationship, and yet it often works. Both signs are from the Earth element, so have a common sense approach to life. They have a mutual understanding, and share many interests. Taurus understands and copes well with Virgo's fussy nature, while Virgo revels in the Bull's tidy and artistic qualities. Both sides are committed to achieving lasting material success. There won't be fireworks, and the match may lack a certain 'spiritual' feel, but as that works both ways it may not be a problem. Star rating: *****

Taurus meets Libra

A happy life is important to both these signs and, as they are both ruled by Venus, they share a common understanding, even though they display themselves so differently. Taurus is quieter than Libra but can be decisive, and that's what counts. Libra is interested in absolutely everything, an infectious quality when seen through Taurean eyes. The slightly flighty qualities of Libra may lead to jealousy from the Bull. Not an argumentative relationship and one that often works well. There could be many changes of address for this pair. Star rating: ****

Taurus meets Scorpio

Scorpio is deep – very deep – which may be a problem, because Taurus doesn't wear its heart on its sleeve either. It might be difficult for this pair to get together, because neither are naturally inclined to make the first move. Taurus stands in awe of the power and intensity of the Scorpio mind, while the Scorpion is interested in the Bull's affable and friendly qualities, so an enduring relationship could be forged if the couple ever get round to talking. Both are lovers of home and family, which will help to cement a relationship. Star rating: **

Taurus meets Sagittarius

On first impression, Taurus may not like Sagittarius, who may seem brash, and even common, when viewed through the Bull's refined eyes. But there is hope of success because the two signs have so much to offer each other. The Archer is enthralled by the Taurean's natural poise and beauty, while Taurus always needs more basic confidence, which is no problem to Sagittarius who has plenty to spare. Both signs love to travel. There are certain to be ups and downs, but that doesn't prevent an interesting, inspiring and even exciting combination. Star rating: ***

Taurus meets Capricorn

If not quite a match made in heaven, this comes close. Both signs are earthy in nature and that is a promising start. Capricorn is very practical and can make a Taurean's dreams come true. Both are tidy, like to know what is going to happen in a day-to-day sense, and are steady and committed. Taurus loves refinement, which Capricorn accepts and even helps to create. A good prognosis for material success rounds off a relationship that could easily stay the course. The only thing missing is a genuine sense of humour. Star rating: ****

Taurus meets Aquarius

In any relationship of which Aquarius is a part, surprises abound. It is difficult for Taurus to understand the soul-searching, adventurous, changeable Aquarian, but on the positive side, the Bull is adaptable and can respond well to a dose of excitement. Aquarians are kind and react well to the same quality coming back at them. Both are friendly, capable of deep affection and basically quite creative. Unfortunately, though, Taurus simply doesn't know what makes Aquarius tick, which could lead to hidden feelings of isolation. Star rating: **

Taurus meets Pisces

No problem here, unless both parties come from the quieter side of their respective signs. Most of the time Taurus and Pisces would live comfortably together, offering mutual support and deep regard. Taurus can offer the personal qualities that Pisces craves, whilst Pisces understands and copes with the Bull's slightly stubborn qualities. Taurus is likely to travel in Piscean company, so there is a potential for wide-ranging experiences and variety which is essential. There will be some misunderstandings, mainly because Pisces is so deep, but that won't prevent their enduring happiness. Star rating: ***

Taurus meets Aries

This match has been known to work very well. Aries brings dynamism and ambition, while Taurus has the patience to see things through logically. Such complementary views work equally well in a relationship or in an office environment. There is mutual respect, but sometimes a lack of total understanding. The romantic needs of each sign are quite different, but both are still fulfilled. Taurus and Aries can live easily in domestic harmony which is very important, but, interestingly, Aries may be the loser in battles of will. Star rating: ***

VENUS:
THE PLANET OF LOVE

If you look up at the sky around sunset or sunrise you will often see Venus in close attendance to the Sun. It is arguably one of the most beautiful sights of all and there is little wonder that historically it became associated with the goddess of love. But although Venus does play an important part in the way you view love and in the way others see you romantically, this is only one of the spheres of influence that it enjoys in your overall character.

Venus has a part to play in the more cultured side of your life and has much to do with your appreciation of art, literature, music and general creativity. Even the way you look is responsive to the part of the zodiac that Venus occupied at the start of your life, though this fact is also down to your Sun sign and Ascending sign. If, at the time you were born, Venus occupied one of the more gregarious zodiac signs, you will be more likely to wear your heart on your sleeve, as well as to be more attracted to entertainment, social gatherings and good company. If on the other hand Venus occupied a quiet zodiac sign at the time of your birth, you would tend to be more retiring and less willing to shine in public situations.

It's good to know what part the planet Venus plays in your life, for it can have a great bearing on the way you appear to the rest of the world and since we all have to mix with others, you can learn to make the very best of what Venus has to offer you.

One of the great complications in the past has always been trying to establish exactly what zodiac position Venus enjoyed when you were born, because the planet is notoriously difficult to track. However, we have solved that problem by creating a table that is exclusive to your Sun sign, which you will find on the following page.

Establishing your Venus sign could not be easier. Just look up the year of your birth on the following page and you will see a sign of the zodiac. This was the sign that Venus occupied in the period covered by your sign in that year. If Venus occupied more than one sign during the period, this is indicated by the date on which the sign changed, and the name of the new sign. For instance, if you were born in 1950, Venus was in Pisces until the 5th May, after which time it was in Aries. If you were born before 5th May your Venus sign is Pisces, if you were born on or after 5th May, your Venus sign is Aries. Once you have established the position of Venus at the time of your birth, you can then look in the pages which follow to see how this has a bearing on your life as a whole.

1910 PISCES / 7.5 ARIES
1911 GEMINI / 13.5 CANCER
1912 ARIES / 8.5 TAURUS
1913 TAURUS / 30.4 ARIES
1914 TAURUS / 2.5 GEMINI
1915 PISCES / 27.4 ARIES
1916 GEMINI / 6.5 CANCER
1917 TAURUS / 16.5 GEMINI
1918 PISCES / 7.5 ARIES
1919 GEMINI / 13.5 CANCER
1920 ARIES / 7.5 TAURUS
1921 TAURUS / 27.4 ARIES
1922 TAURUS / 2.5 GEMINI
1923 PISCES / 27.4 ARIES
1924 GEMINI / 7.5 CANCER
1925 TAURUS / 16.5 GEMINI
1926 PISCES / 6.5 ARIES
1927 GEMINI / 12.5 CANCER
1928 ARIES / 6.5 TAURUS
1929 TAURUS / 24.4 ARIES
1930 TAURUS / 1.5 GEMINI
1931 PISCES / 26.4 ARIES
1932 GEMINI / 8.5 CANCER
1933 TAURUS / 15.5 GEMINI
1934 PISCES / 6.5 ARIES
1935 GEMINI / 12.5 CANCER
1936 ARIES / 6.5 TAURUS
1937 TAURUS / 21.4 ARIES
1938 TAURUS / 1.5 GEMINI
1939 PISCES / 26.4 ARIES
1940 GEMINI / 9.5 CANCER
1941 TAURUS / 14.5 GEMINI
1942 PISCES / 6.5 ARIES
1943 GEMINI / 11.5 CANCER
1944 ARIES / 6.5 TAURUS
1945 ARIES
1946 TAURUS / 30.4 GEMINI
1947 PISCES / 25.4 ARIES
1948 GEMINI / 9.5 CANCER
1949 TAURUS / 14.5 GEMINI
1950 PISCES / 5.5 ARIES
1951 GEMINI / 11.5 CANCER
1952 ARIES / 5.5 TAURUS
1953 ARIES
1954 TAURUS / 29.4 GEMINI
1955 PISCES / 25.4 ARIES
1956 GEMINI / 10.5 CANCER
1957 TAURUS / 13.5 GEMINI
1958 PISCES / 5.5 ARIES
1959 GEMINI / 10.5 CANCER

1960 ARIES / 4.5 TAURUS
1961 ARIES
1962 TAURUS / 28.4 GEMINI
1963 PISCES / 24.4 ARIES
1964 GEMINI / 11.5 CANCER
1965 TAURUS / 13.5 GEMINI
1966 PISCES / 5.5 ARIES
1967 GEMINI / 10.5 CANCER
1968 ARIES / 4.5 TAURUS
1969 ARIES
1970 TAURUS / 27.4 GEMINI
1971 PISCES / 24.4 ARIES
1972 GEMINI / 12.5 CANCER
1973 TAURUS / 12.5 GEMINI
1974 PISCES / 4.5 ARIES
1975 GEMINI / 9.5 CANCER
1976 ARIES / 3.5 TAURUS
1977 ARIES
1978 TAURUS / 27.4 GEMINI
1979 PISCES / 23.4 ARIES
1980 GEMINI / 13.5 CANCER
1981 TAURUS / 12.5 GEMINI
1982 PISCES / 4.5 ARIES
1983 GEMINI / 9.5 CANCER
1984 ARIES / 3.5 TAURUS
1985 ARIES
1986 TAURUS / 26.4 GEMINI
1987 PISCES / 23.4 ARIES
1988 GEMINI / 15.5 CANCER
1989 TAURUS / 11.5 GEMINI
1990 PISCES / 4.5 ARIES
1991 GEMINI / 8.5 CANCER
1992 ARIES / 2.5 TAURUS
1993 ARIES
1994 TAURUS / 26.4 GEMINI
1995 PISCES / 22.4 ARIES
1996 GEMINI / 15.5 CANCER
1997 TAURUS / 11.5 GEMINI
1998 PISCES / 3.5 ARIES
1999 GEMINI / 8.5 CANCER
2000 ARIES / 2.5 TAURUS
2001 ARIES
2002 TAURUS / 26.4 GEMINI
2003 PISCES / 22.4 ARIES
2004 GEMINI / 15.5 CANCER
2005 TAURUS / 11.5 GEMINI
2006 PISCES / 3.5 ARIES
2007 GEMINI / 8.5 CANCER
2008 ARIES / 2.5 TAURUS

VENUS THROUGH THE ZODIAC SIGNS

Venus in Aries

mongst other things, the position of Venus in Aries indicates a
ondness for travel, music and all creative pursuits. Your nature
ends to be affectionate and you would try not to create confusion
r difficulty for others if it could be avoided. Many people with this
lanetary position have a great love of the theatre, and mental
imulation is of the greatest importance. Early romantic
tachments are common with Venus in Aries, so it is very important
o establish a genuine sense of romantic continuity. Early marriage
not recommended, especially if it is based on sympathy. You may
ve your heart a little too readily on occasions.

Venus in Taurus

ou are capable of very deep feelings and your emotions tend to last
r a very long time. This makes you a trusting partner and lover,
hose constancy is second to none. In life you are precise and careful
d always try to do things the right way. Although this means an
dered life, which you are comfortable with, it can also lead you to
e rather too fussy for your own good. Despite your pleasant nature,
ou are very fixed in your opinions and quite able to speak your
ind. Others are attracted to you and historical astrologers always
oted this position of Venus as being very fortunate in terms of
arriage. However, if you find yourself involved in a failed
lationship, it could take you a long time to trust again.

Venus in Gemini

s with all associations related to Gemini, you tend to be quite
rsatile, anxious for change and intelligent in your dealings with
e world at large. You may gain money from more than one source
t you are equally good at spending it. There is an inference here
at you are a good communicator, via either the written or the
oken word, and you love to be in the company of interesting
ople. Always on the look-out for culture, you may also be very
nd of music, and love to indulge the curious and cultured side of
ur nature. In romance you tend to have more than one
ationship and could find yourself associated with someone who
s previously been a friend or even a distant relative.

Venus in Cancer

You often stay close to home because you are very fond of family and enjoy many of your most treasured moments when you are with those you love. Being naturally sympathetic, you will always do anything you can to support those around you, even people you hardly know at all. This charitable side of your nature is your most noticeable trait and is one of the reasons why others are naturally so fond of you. Being receptive and in some cases even psychic, you can see through to the soul of most of those with whom you come into contact. You may not commence too many romantic attachments but when you do give your heart, it tends to be unconditionally.

Venus in Leo

It must become quickly obvious to almost anyone you meet that you are kind, sympathetic and yet determined enough to stand up for anyone or anything that is truly important to you. Bright and sunny, you warm the world with your natural enthusiasm and would rarely do anything to hurt those around you, or at least not intentionally. In romance you are ardent and sincere, though some may find your style just a little overpowering. Gains come through your contacts with other people and this could be especially true with regard to romance, for love and money often come hand in hand for those who were born with Venus in Leo. People claim to understand you, though you are more complex than you seem.

Venus in Virgo

Your nature could well be fairly quiet no matter what your Sun sign might be, though this fact often manifests itself as an inner peace and would not prevent you from being basically sociable. Some delays and even the odd disappointment in love cannot be ruled out with this planetary position, though it's a fact that you will usually find the happiness you look for in the end. Catapulting yourself into romantic entanglements that you know to be rather ill-advised not sensible, and it would be better to wait before you committed yourself exclusively to any one person. It is the essence of your nature to serve the world at large and through doing so it is possible that you will attract money at some stage in your life.

Venus in Libra

Venus is very comfortable in Libra and bestows upon those people who have this planetary position a particular sort of kindness that is easy to recognise. This is a very good position for all sorts of friendships and also for romantic attachments that usually bring much joy into your life. Few individuals with Venus in Libra would avoid marriage and since you are capable of great depths of love, it is likely that you will find a contented personal life. You like to mix with people of integrity and intelligence but don't take kindly to scruffy surroundings or work that means getting your hands too dirty. Careful speculation, good business dealings and money through marriage all seem fairly likely.

Venus in Scorpio

You are quite open and tend to spend money quite freely, even on those occasions when you don't have very much. Although your intentions are always good, there are times when you get yourself in to the odd scrape and this can be particularly true when it comes to romance, which you may come to late or from a rather unexpected direction. Certainly you have the power to be happy and to make others contented on the way, but you find the odd stumbling block in your journey through life and it could seem that you have to work harder than those around you. As a result of this, you gain a much deeper understanding of the true value of personal happiness than many people ever do, and are likely to achieve true contentment in the end.

Venus in Sagittarius

You are lighthearted, cheerful and always able to see the funny side of any situation. These facts enhance your popularity, which is especially high with members of the opposite sex. You should never have to look too far to find romantic interest in your life, though it is just possible that you might be too willing to commit yourself before you are certain that the person in question is right for you. Part of the problem here extends to other areas of life too. The fact is that you like variety in everything and so can tire of situations that fail to offer it. All the same, if you choose wisely and learn to understand your restless side, then great happiness can be yours.

Venus in Capricorn

The most notable trait that comes from Venus in this position is that it makes you trustworthy and able to take on all sorts of responsibilities in life. People are instinctively fond of you and love you all the more because you are always ready to help those who are in any form of need. Social and business popularity can be yours and there is a magnetic quality to your nature that is particularly attractive in a romantic sense. Anyone who wants a partner for lover, a spouse and a good friend too would almost certainly look in your direction. Constancy is the hallmark of your nature and unfaithfulness would go right against the grain. You might sometimes be a little too trusting.

Venus in Aquarius

This location of Venus offers a fondness for travel and a desire to try out something new at every possible opportunity. You are extremely easy to get along with and tend to have many friends from varied backgrounds, classes and inclinations. You like to live a distinct sort of life and gain a great deal from moving about, both in a career sense and with regard to your home. It is not out of the question that you could form a romantic attachment to someone who comes from far away or be attracted to a person of a distinctly artistic and original nature. What you cannot stand is jealousy, for you have friends of both sexes and would want to keep things that way.

Venus in Pisces

The first thing people tend to notice about you is your wonderful warm smile. Being very charitable by nature you will do anything to help others, even if you don't know them well. Much of your life may be spent sorting out situations for other people, but it is very important to feel that you are living for yourself too. In the main you remain cheerful, and tend to be quite attractive to members of the opposite sex. Where romantic attachments are concerned, you could be drawn to people who are significantly older or younger than yourself or to someone with a unique career or point of view. It might be best for you to avoid marrying whilst you are still very young.

TAURUS:
2007 DIARY PAGES

October

2007

1 MONDAY
Moon Age Day 19   Moon Sign Gemini

Try to avoid being over-critical today or you will slow down your natural tendency towards progress. With Mars in your solar third house there is just the chance that your remarks to others will be barbed or else a little caustic. Some forward thinking on your part can help you to prevent unfortunate situations occurring.

2 TUESDAY
Moon Age Day 20   Moon Sign Gemini

There are signs that you could be somewhat preoccupied with personal matters, a fact that might detract from your ability to cope with professional or practical pressures. What isn't in doubt is your romantic attitude. This tends to be very strong at the moment and you are in a good position to offer just the right compliments.

3 WEDNESDAY
Moon Age Day 21   Moon Sign Cancer

You have a natural talent for communicating at the moment, and even if you are still telling it the way it is, you should be able to get your message across with very little difficulty. There is room for a possible change of direction in an important area of your life so don't be too definite about anything!

4 THURSDAY
Moon Age Day 22   Moon Sign Cancer

You can advance professionally by sticking to specific ambitions, even if it seems that others have different ideas about what you should do. There is a strong tendency for you to win through in the end, so a little adversity should prove to be nothing but a temporary distraction. A day to keep your eyes on your ultimate objectives.

5 FRIDAY
Moon Age Day 23   Moon Sign Leo

Seeing the point of view that others are putting forward may not be very easy for you on this autumn Friday. Instead of instinctively becoming defensive, your best approach is to try to stretch your mind towards possibilities you might not have considered before. Casual conversations can enable you to reach great realisations.

6 SATURDAY
Moon Age Day 24   Moon Sign Leo

This is an excellent time for the exchange of ideas and for promoting any causes that are really important to you. Some Taurus subjects could have been feeling a little off-colour over the last couple of days, and if you are one of them chances are that you are now back on the road to full recovery.

7 SUNDAY
Moon Age Day 25   Moon Sign Leo

It's worth seeking out the best of company today, and you need to make the very best of the favourable social trends that surround you. It doesn't matter if some jobs at home have to wait. What proves to be most important right now is your ability to get on well no matter what you decide to undertake.

8 MONDAY
Moon Age Day 26   Moon Sign Virgo

There is no reason why you should not be getting ahead very well with some of your plans, and the week ahead can be generally good from a work point of view. Any minor frustrations early this week needn't get in your way, but you might have to talk quite harshly to someone in the family.

9 TUESDAY
Moon Age Day 27   Moon Sign Virgo

Your personal charisma can be used to your distinct advantage at the moment. Words spill from your mouth like honey and you might also be more humorous than usual. People like to have you around at the best of times, but you can make sure they are especially keen to enjoy your company right now.

10 WEDNESDAY   *Moon Age Day 28   Moon Sign Libra*

Even if there are a number of tedious jobs to get out of the way today, you can approach them with a very positive frame of mind and so needn't be in the least worried about them. Casual comments made by others may lead you to believe that you are high in their estimation, both professionally and personally.

11 THURSDAY   *Moon Age Day 0   Moon Sign Libra*

Avoid making decisions too rapidly and be willing to look at the bigger picture. This is especially true when it comes to your personal life and to romance. You need to be careful if there are fascinating people around at present, as you could be so dazzled by their presence that you forget something important.

12 FRIDAY   ☿   *Moon Age Day 1   Moon Sign Libra*

You are able to finish the working week on a positive note, but you may already notice that things generally are slowing down somewhat. Beware of overcommitting yourself for the weekend ahead because the Moon is moving into your opposite sign later today. Slow and steady definitely does win the race for Saturday and Sunday.

13 SATURDAY   ☿   *Moon Age Day 2   Moon Sign Scorpio*

Avoid getting yourself into a pickle by ignoring advice that you instinctively know might be quite suspect. You would be wise to make up your mind on the basis of your own common sense and a little Taurean intuition. Where possible, stick to social matters and leave important decisions until after the weekend.

14 SUNDAY   ☿   *Moon Age Day 3   Moon Sign Scorpio*

Don't be afraid to reserve some time today for solitude. You would be much better off taking a few hours to yourself because using your charisma and charm may not be as easy as usual. If you don't commit yourself to anything specific you are less likely to disappoint someone when you feel you have to pull out.

15 MONDAY ☿ *Moon Age Day 4*   *Moon Sign Sagittarius*

The Moon moves on, just in time for you to address what looks like being another quite busy week. Things that happen behind the scenes could be of specific interest to you, and it is certain that you can be right on the ball again when it comes to making the right decision at the most appropriate time.

16 TUESDAY ☿ *Moon Age Day 5*   *Moon Sign Sagittarius*

The major emphasis right now is on play, particularly if you really don't feel too much like working for hours at a stretch. You can be funny, enthusiastic and anxious to enjoy yourself, but you are not anywhere near as committed to the practical aspects of life as is usually the case for hard-working Taurus.

17 WEDNESDAY ☿ *Moon Age Day 6*   *Moon Sign Sagittarius*

You can share interesting ideas with others today and should not be too alarmed if you don't seem to be pushing forward at quite the pace you had anticipated. Sometimes you have to spoil yourself and a little luxury now will set you up for busier times to come closer to the end of the year.

18 THURSDAY ☿ *Moon Age Day 7*   *Moon Sign Capricorn*

The Moon moving into your solar ninth house can prove to be something of an eye-opener. Your views on life may well be changed significantly, and possibly all because of the casual comments of other people. There are certainly surprises in store, though most of them ought to be fortunate ones.

19 FRIDAY ☿ *Moon Age Day 8*   *Moon Sign Capricorn*

If you have decided on a particular course of action today it would be advisable to stick to it. Jumping around from foot to foot might give others the wrong impression about the way your nature works. It is possible that you are being carefully watched at the moment, so try to give the best impression possible.

20 SATURDAY ☿ *Moon Age Day 9   Moon Sign Aquarius*

When it comes to mixing with others you should now be at your very best. By being both talkative and interesting you shouldn't have any difficulty at all making the best of impressions. If you are a weekend worker you may find that your usual routines are changed, but if you take this fact in your stride you can be the winner.

21 SUNDAY ☿ *Moon Age Day 10   Moon Sign Aquarius*

People tend to look to you as an authority figure at the best of times, mainly because you are so capable. However, they are really relying on you at present and you will need to be as wise as Solomon if you are going to please everyone. It's pointless trying – but that's Taurus!

22 MONDAY ☿ *Moon Age Day 11   Moon Sign Pisces*

You can afford to feel happy and confident today and should know exactly what to do to get your own way. This isn't entirely selfish because you can do so much for others on the way. There is little to prevent you from getting where you want to be in a professional sense this week but some care may be necessary in romance.

23 TUESDAY ☿ *Moon Age Day 12   Moon Sign Pisces*

Your strength lies in finding the happy medium between committing yourself to the needs of relationships and the demands being made of you in a practical sense. It might be necessary to split your time carefully, and overconfidence of any sort would be a mistake under present trends. Finances can be strengthened around now.

24 WEDNESDAY ☿ *Moon Age Day 13   Moon Sign Pisces*

A day to make an effort to communicate in as clear and concise a manner as you can. If you don't, misunderstandings are possible, and these will be of no use to you whatsoever. Routines should be easily dealt with but you may also feel a longing need to be breaking the bounds of convention.

25 THURSDAY ☿ *Moon Age Day 14 Moon Sign Aries*

Your burning desire to get ahead may now be rewarded. It looks as though you can get your ideas taken on board in a number of different areas, and as long as you keep your nose to the grindstone you should be in for some pleasant surprises. Your life seems to be filled with interesting characters at this time.

26 FRIDAY ☿ *Moon Age Day 15 Moon Sign Aries*

Good luck is there for the taking in chance encounters, and there is no reason at all why you should not find profit at the end of this week. The Moon moves into your zodiac sign later today and offers a positive sort of weekend and one during which you make your own choices in life.

27 SATURDAY ☿ *Moon Age Day 16 Moon Sign Taurus*

Fresh initiatives are available all the time now, and some of them arrive from the most surprising directions. You may not be committing yourself to hard work, particularly if there is plenty happening on the social scene. This is a day from which you get the most if you respond to instant planning.

28 SUNDAY ☿ *Moon Age Day 17 Moon Sign Taurus*

Trends suggest that strong personalities of one sort or another predominate in your life now, but all of them can contribute to an even more dynamic approach from you personally. When you pit your wits against the most intelligent people you know this merely allows you to confirm your own present confidence in yourself.

29 MONDAY ☿ *Moon Age Day 18 Moon Sign Gemini*

Avoid confrontations at the start of this week and as much as possible stick solidly to what you know. There are plenty of opportunities to prove yourself, but you do so best when you are definitely on firm ground. Confidence continues to grow, but may be dented somewhat if you reach too far for your own good.

30 TUESDAY ☿ Moon Age Day 19 Moon Sign Gemini

Romantic developments are highlighted for you today and you have what it takes to make the best possible impression on someone you care about deeply. Just be yourself and don't avoid nerves to creep in when it matters the most. There is no need to put on any kind of show.

31 WEDNESDAY ☿ Moon Age Day 20 Moon Sign Cancer

You have excellent powers of communication at your disposal under present trends, and this is clearly the time to go for something you really want. Personal attachments could still predominate, and although there are still gains available in practical matters, you might decide you want to mix and mingle as much as possible.

⑧ November

2007

1 THURSDAY   ☿   *Moon Age Day 21*   *Moon Sign Cancer*

Disagreements over the most mundane of matters might seem to take up a great deal of your time around now. The secret is not to get involved. Stick to what you know and don't be drawn into discussions or arguments that you know are a waste of time. A day to keep abreast of news, especially at a local level.

2 FRIDAY   ☿   *Moon Age Day 22*   *Moon Sign Leo*

Matters on the domestic scene are very well accented at the moment, and although you may be forced to respond to matters out there in the wider world, this is not what you particularly want to do. Family members could now give you good reason to be proud of them by scoring significant personal successes.

3 SATURDAY   *Moon Age Day 23*   *Moon Sign Leo*

In social situations you gain through a mixture of diplomacy and your natural winning charm. The weekend offers diversions of many different sorts, and the only real fly in the ointment is that you can't be everywhere at once. You can afford to opt for a change of scene whenever this is offered to you.

4 SUNDAY   *Moon Age Day 24*   *Moon Sign Virgo*

Trends suggest that your need to be the centre of attention is paramount at the moment, so you might be doing everything you can to be noticed. This might prove to be something of a problem on occasions, particulary if those around you feel exactly the same. It's a sort of competition that you can't always win.

5 MONDAY
Moon Age Day 25   Moon Sign Virg

You can make sure that relationships are especially rewardin
around now. There are some fortunate planetary positions about fo
you, but none more so than the present position of the Sun. If you
opinion is being sought on all fronts, you should be feeling prett
important. If nothing else this can boost your ego.

6 TUESDAY
Moon Age Day 26   Moon Sign Libr

There might be a new love interest on the horizon for thos
Taureans who are between attachments at the moment. In order fo
this to happen you will have to put yourself in the way of intereste
parties. Social trends are presently positive, and even if you remai
busy in a practical sense you have much social energy too.

7 WEDNESDAY
Moon Age Day 27   Moon Sign Libr

Progress is possible through work and through a strong sense c
efficiency. It isn't so much what you do that matters at the momen
but the attitude you take towards it. Once you are away from th
practical world you shouldn't be afraid to display a highly origina
approach towards all social and romantic situations.

8 THURSDAY
Moon Age Day 28   Moon Sign Libr

Developing work skills are worth exploring because you seem t
have skills at your fingertips right now that set you apart in som
way. It should also be plain that you are a born organiser at presen
and that you will expect others to follow your lead withou
question. Some hope!

9 FRIDAY
Moon Age Day 0   Moon Sign Scorpi

This might be as good a time as any to slow things down. Since th
lunar low is upon you there isn't much point in flogging yourself t
death, and you can achieve far more by watching and waiting for
while. In the meantime, you may decide to catch up on som
reading and perhaps spend a few hours improving skills that nee
attention.

10 SATURDAY   *Moon Age Day 1   Moon Sign Scorpio*

Even if you notice an increase in family pressure this is something you need to turn away from if at all possible. Spend a few hours doing whatever pleases you and don't be too keen to get involved in issues that cannot easily be resolved. In particular, beware of getting involved in arguments.

11 SUNDAY   *Moon Age Day 2   Moon Sign Sagittarius*

You seem to have a heightened curiosity, and now that the lunar low is out of the way you might be very keen to turn your attention to more progressive concerns. One thing you should avoid is asking personal questions of anyone who may get rather upset as a result.

12 MONDAY   *Moon Age Day 3   Moon Sign Sagittarius*

It appears that you are very socially oriented at present and that you simply cannot get enough of being in the company of people you find stimulating and attractive. This is one time of the year at which you could promote a little jealousy without having any intention of doing so. Care is needed.

13 TUESDAY   *Moon Age Day 4   Moon Sign Sagittarius*

Even unexpected contacts can bring good news, and it would be worth spending some time today getting in touch with people you don't hear from very often. Even if you remain essentially busy in all practical matters, you can afford to put aside some time to plan for the end of the year and the Christmas period.

14 WEDNESDAY   *Moon Age Day 5   Moon Sign Capricorn*

Trends encourage you to be very outgoing for the next couple of days, and you can make great gains as a result of your desire to talk to anyone and everyone. With an essentially carefree attitude and a strong desire to push the bounds of the possible, few people can ignore your refreshing and stimulating nature.

15 THURSDAY   *Moon Age Day 6   Moon Sign Capricorn*

If you decide you want to be helpful, you might now be spending quite a lot of your time sorting out the difficulties and practical problems of others. The charitable side of your nature definitely predominates at this time and you needn't be shy of interfering in situations if you know you can do some good.

16 FRIDAY   *Moon Age Day 7   Moon Sign Aquarius*

In all professional matters you should now back your own instincts rather than following the rather odd advice that seems to be coming from other directions. It ought to be possible to do your own thing without upsetting others as a result. Present trends tend to enhance your romantic side.

17 SATURDAY   *Moon Age Day 8   Moon Sign Aquarius*

You probably need lots of variety and the stimulation that comes from ringing the changes this weekend. It's not the sort of period during which you should hang around your home too much. Rather you need to be on the move, possibly taking with you someone who thinks you are wonderful.

18 SUNDAY   *Moon Age Day 9   Moon Sign Aquarius*

You will be quite amazed to discover just how popular you can become at the moment. As a result it might be difficult to fulfil everyone's expectations. Sunday is not just about doing things but usually offers something of a rest. Nothing could be further from the truth this time around. Simply try to be organised.

19 MONDAY   *Moon Age Day 10   Moon Sign Pisces*

You have a naturally diplomatic attitude as a rule and this quality of your nature is really enhanced under present trends. As a result you show yourself to be an excellent mediator and shouldn't be easily fazed by having to wade into some difficult situations. People automatically tend to follow your advice.

20 TUESDAY
Moon Age Day 11   Moon Sign Pisces

Matters associated with either business or simply the practical issues of life may well keep you on the go now, and there probably won't be all that much time to spend on yourself. At least try to set part of the evening aside so that you can spoil yourself in some way. A little relaxation is very important at the moment.

21 WEDNESDAY
Moon Age Day 12   Moon Sign Aries

Perhaps not everyone has your best interests at heart today, and you need to be careful before you take any advice that might not be as impartial as it seems. In particular you should avoid signing anything until you have read the small print. A day to stick with people you know you can trust and whom you have known for a long time.

22 THURSDAY
Moon Age Day 13   Moon Sign Aries

The Moon is still in your solar twelfth house, so you can make this a quieter sort of day during which you can find plenty of time to weigh up the pros and cons of any given situation. By tomorrow things could change significantly, so why not take full advantage of having some room to breath?

23 FRIDAY
Moon Age Day 14   Moon Sign Taurus

This is one of the best days of the month during which you can really make an impression on life. Arriving at decisions should take only seconds, and you will be pushing ahead whilst others are still wandering around in a daze. If you want to get ahead you need to concentrate all your efforts now.

24 SATURDAY
Moon Age Day 15   Moon Sign Taurus

You should be able to find plenty of excitement in your life during the present interlude, and the lunar high gives you every incentive to get ahead and to stay there. The weekend offers scope for change and diversity, as well as a chance to try out something that has probably been in your mind for quite a time.

25 SUNDAY   *Moon Age Day 16   Moon Sign Gemini*

You should have all the help you need in personal affairs – in fact it might be suggested that people are rather more helpful than you might have wished. Try to be diplomatic and to accept their assistance without being critical. Taurus can be just a little outspoken on occasions, and that's something you should avoid today.

26 MONDAY   *Moon Age Day 17   Moon Sign Gemini*

There are great opportunities about to get ahead with work today, but you may not get very far if you insist on going it alone all the time. Trends assist you to persuade anyone you have helped in the past to return the favour and you are in a perfect position to gain ground as a result of their desire to give you a leg up.

27 TUESDAY   *Moon Age Day 18   Moon Sign Cancer*

When it comes to solving problems of one sort of another you are now in the best of all positions. Astrologically speaking, you have what it takes to be both critical and open-minded. This proves to be a formidable combination when it comes to being ahead of the game. Stand by the decisions you decide to make.

28 WEDNESDAY   *Moon Age Day 19   Moon Sign Cancer*

Avoid making mistakes that come about as a result of either fatigue or an inability to get yourself into exactly the right frame of mind. You would now be better off dealing with situations that you instinctively know you can get on top of. Someone you haven't seen for ages could well be turning up again.

29 THURSDAY   *Moon Age Day 20   Moon Sign Leo*

You can now achieve a peaceful and relaxing interlude, and shouldn't be fazed if someone in your immediate vicinity is behaving in a rather strange manner. The pull of nostalgia may be hard to avoid, perhaps because of the time of year and the proximity of the festive season.

30 FRIDAY

Moon Age Day 21   Moon Sign Leo

You may need to unravel a complicated personal issue ahead of the weekend, and would be better off addressing the situation as soon as possible. Arguing for your limitations mere means coming face to face with them. Although it's important to face your demons, you might want to keep at least some of them locked up for today.

8

December
2007

1 SATURDAY
Moon Age Day 22   Moon Sign Virgo

The Moon now moves into your solar fifth house, assisting you to stir things up as far as your love life is concerned. You certainly have potential to make yourself the centre of attention during the weekend and won't mind a bit if people are putting you on some sort of pedestal. This can be a very stimulating sort of day.

2 SUNDAY
Moon Age Day 23   Moon Sign Virgo

Unpredictable events come thick and fast under present influences, and as long as you see the gains that arrive with them all should be well. Someone new may be knocking at the door of your life – maybe a friend of a friend. A new phase is about to open for some Taureans and it's one that offers great possibilities.

3 MONDAY
Moon Age Day 24   Moon Sign Virgo

It is clear that you should now have the energy and desire to get on in life. The only potential problem is if others don't. Instead of trying to drag them along behind you it might be more sensible simply to do your own thing for a few hours. You can also perk up your social life no end this week.

4 TUESDAY
Moon Age Day 25   Moon Sign Libra

Impulsive thinking can lead to both mistakes and misunderstandings. Not only is it important to mull things over carefully, you also need to explain your opinions and ideas fully. Once you have done so you should be able to attract all the help you need – some of which comes from very unexpected directions.

5 WEDNESDAY   *Moon Age Day 26   Moon Sign Libra*

Beware of becoming distracted from practical necessities today, no matter how attractive life looks in other directions. Once you have dealt with important matters you can do more or less whatever you wish, but in the early part of the day at least it is vital that you deal with situations as and when they occur.

6 THURSDAY   *Moon Age Day 27   Moon Sign Scorpio*

If not everyone seems to be equally responsive now, you can put most of this down to the arrival of the lunar low. It might actually be good to please yourself for a couple of days and to spend time thinking about how you want to proceed. What might not seem too attractive under present trends will be necessary social commitments.

7 FRIDAY   *Moon Age Day 28   Moon Sign Scorpio*

This is probably not the best time to commit yourself to anything new or to jobs that require your full attention. The fact is that you could run out of steam quicker than usual and in any case you want to spend a few hours simply pleasing yourself. You can summon up your energy again before very long, but in the meantime can afford a break.

8 SATURDAY   *Moon Age Day 29   Moon Sign Scorpio*

The start of today is likely to be as quiet as Thursday and Friday turned out to be, but you can hot things up as the hours advance. The most notable planetary position right now is Venus in your solar seventh house. This makes romantic developments the most important area on which to concentrate.

9 SUNDAY   *Moon Age Day 0   Moon Sign Sagittarius*

Though it is clear that you are mentally alert at this time you might also show a tendency to be short-tempered. This will be especially true if you are faced with people who seem to be deliberately ignoring your advice. Where is that famous Taurean patience? It could seem to have disappeared for the moment.

10 MONDAY
Moon Age Day 1   Moon Sign Sagittarius

A day to trust your hunches and follow them wherever they lead. Your intuitive powers are now at their highest and you shouldn't go far wrong if you stick to doing what seems right for most of today. A little romantic interlude is possible later in the day, and this might have distinctly seasonal overtones.

11 TUESDAY
Moon Age Day 2   Moon Sign Capricorn

The swift pace you set yourself today might be too much for a few other people – something that could well occur frequently during December. You would be wise to stay as patient as you can, though it's fine if you feel the need to proceed in any case. Your concern for the underdog tends to strengthen as the day advances.

12 WEDNESDAY
Moon Age Day 3   Moon Sign Capricorn

Try to express your ideas as patiently as you can. If there's one thing that could get your goat at the moment it is the fact that some of the people you have to deal with seem so dense. The problem may not be so much in their comprehension but in your inability to put your message across as well as you might.

13 THURSDAY
Moon Age Day 4   Moon Sign Capricorn

You should be feeling a good deal more settled inside yourself as the Moon comes racing to your aid. Some of the impulsive tendencies of the last few days should disappear and you find yourself calmer and more responsive. It might be said that the true Taurean qualities are now more in evidence.

14 FRIDAY
Moon Age Day 5   Moon Sign Aquarius

Venus brings a potential lift in one-to-one relationships and offers you the chance to express yourself fully in romantic matters. Social situations now suit you better and there is a great ability to mix business with pleasure so effectively that gains are likely to result. Don't waste time today on irrelevant details.

15 SATURDAY   *Moon Age Day 6   Moon Sign Aquarius*

You might feel compelled to change your surroundings this weekend because you show a definite restless streak. This could be something of a problem when Christmas is so close and there is so much to be arranged. Maybe you can find ways to split your time and that way you can please yourself and everyone else too.

16 SUNDAY   *Moon Age Day 7   Moon Sign Pisces*

You are entering a distinctly dynamic social period and there are great challenges about when it comes to further developing your abilities to get on with people. It is clear that you have what it takes to be popular with a significant cross-section of individuals – but not everyone!

17 MONDAY   *Moon Age Day 8   Moon Sign Pisces*

You seem to have the mind of a detective today. Trends indicate that your curiosity is roused and you want to know the reason for everything. With plenty to go for in a financial sense you could be better off now than you have been throughout December so far, but it's possible that money will also pass through your hands very quickly.

18 TUESDAY   *Moon Age Day 9   Moon Sign Aries*

You may feel inspired to make vital changes, especially at home. However, this might be a time during which you should ask yourself if these are appropriate. With Christmas just around the corner and lots to arrange, this probably isn't the best period for turning everything upside down in other ways.

19 WEDNESDAY   *Moon Age Day 10   Moon Sign Aries*

You have scope to enlarge your circle of social and business contacts under present trends. As a result you might meet someone you find to be particularly attractive. What you decide to do about this situation remains to be seen, but this is certainly not a time to engender jealousy in others.

20 THURSDAY   *Moon Age Day 11   Moon Sign Tauru.*

The Moon moves back into your zodiac sign and brings with it the most forward-looking period during the whole of this month. You should be right on the ball with your hunches and well able to tackle half a dozen different jobs at the same time. The only slight word of warning once again is that others may not be able to keep up.

21 FRIDAY   *Moon Age Day 12   Moon Sign Tauru*

Even difficult situations can now be turned to your advantage and you can achieve a level of popularity amongst others that is going right off the scale. It's party time for Taurus and the full implications of the Christmas period may only dawn on you now. Make the most of these very positive trends.

22 SATURDAY   *Moon Age Day 13   Moon Sign Gemin*

There isn't any doubt about the fact that you can be very assertive now, and whilst that's fine when it comes to getting what you want from life, there may be people around who are not that inclined to go along with your thinking. In addition to dynamism you also need to cultivate your usual diplomacy.

23 SUNDAY   *Moon Age Day 14   Moon Sign Gemin.*

You have what it takes to attract the good things in life, and you may have news of a specific Christmas gift that has potential to change your life no end. This is also a time during which romance can blossom. Those in established relationships should be in position to increase the heat noticeably.

24 MONDAY   *Moon Age Day 15   Moon Sign Cance*

Travel seems to be positively highlighted now, and even if you are busy finalising details for a real family Christmas, you might also have very itchy feet. Perhaps you intend to visit relatives or friend at a distance. Whatever you decide to do you certainly won't be sitting around all day in the same spot.

25 TUESDAY   *Moon Age Day 16   Moon Sign Cancer*

Christmas Day brings a sense of optimism and freedom that can help you make this an interesting time. Those closest to you could prove to be very attentive and want to do all they can to make you happy. Some of the gains you achieve today are definitely as a result of your own efforts in the past.

26 WEDNESDAY   *Moon Age Day 17   Moon Sign Leo*

There might be an intimate issue around now that definitely does need some attention. Even if you are very busy with social arrangements, you should take the necessary time to get on side with your partner and to discover whether something is bothering them. After that you can continue to party!

27 THURSDAY   *Moon Age Day 18   Moon Sign Leo*

This would be a particularly good day on which to learn something new. Trends could raise your curiosity to fever pitch, and inspire you to spend significant parts of the day asking questions. Beware of getting tied down with family commitments that are quite unnecessary. A timely conversation could solve a few problems.

28 FRIDAY   *Moon Age Day 19   Moon Sign Leo*

Today offers scope to alter your routines and get as much variety into your life as proves to be possible. It is possible that you are already rather fatigued by simply enjoying yourself, and might appreciate some intellectual stimulation. A day to go for gold in sporting activities and to prove something to yourself on the way.

29 SATURDAY   *Moon Age Day 20   Moon Sign Virgo*

This would be a good time to start a new relationship, and it looks as though the Christmas magic is working for some Taureans who are looking for love. Someone you never suspected might be paying you a great deal of attention, and even if you are not interested in them, you should still be flattered.

30 SUNDAY   *Moon Age Day 21   Moon Sign Virg*

You can benefit greatly from a frank exchange of views at this time and have what it takes to speak your mind in almost any situation. What makes matters better is that you can persuade others to listen to what you have to say and to take your opinions on board. Socially speaking you should now be on top form.

31 MONDAY   *Moon Age Day 22   Moon Sign Libr*

Now is the time to get out and about with friends and loved ones and enjoy what today has to offer in terms that gain you nothing but which please you all the same. Standing up for your point of view shouldn't be at all difficult but there might be times today when you ask yourself whether it's worth causing a fuss.

TAURUS:
2008 DIARY PAGES

TAURUS:
2008 IN BRIEF

It's a mixed bag for Taurus at the beginning of the year and you won't be exactly firing on all cylinders throughout the whole of January. On the contrary, you need to show patience and determination if you want to score real successes. This isn't difficult for you and the events of February should demonstrate how well you are doing. Personal issues are not a problem at the start of the year and you build a very comfortable and satisfying home life.

March and April should prove to be slightly more eventful and might bring you to a better understanding of issues that have been on your mind for some time. You think clearly and act positively – so much so that others begin to rely on you more heavily and offer significant support. Your love life should be very interesting at this time.

The arrival of the early summer could find you slightly restless and anxious to make significant changes, especially at home. Don't get hung up with details at work and wherever possible look at the overview of life, rather than dealing with its minutiae. You may show a tendency to worry about family members but if so you will soon come to realise that your concerns are without much foundation. Travel as much as you can during both May and June.

July and August should prove to be quite eventful and the world will be opening up for you more and more. Friends are especially important at this time and you will be extremely social and sociable. This means being put in the spotlight on occasions, and though being out there in the public gaze isn't always your thing you will deal well enough with the situation at this time.

September might see you taking a late holiday and you will certainly be anxious for fresh fields and pastures new. Money matters should be going fairly smoothly and there might even be some cash coming to you that you didn't expect. Both September and October see you relying much more on your intuition than your common sense and some of the decisions you take will surprise those around you.

The last two months of the year, November and December, could turn out to be the most satisfying of all. Arrangements you made earlier will be paying dividends and everything seems to fall into place when it matters the most. The period running up towards Christmas should prove to be eventful and enjoyable and you will relish a contented and happy family life more than anything else. Romance is also on the cards for young or young-at-heart Taurus subjects during the festive season. You can look towards the New Year with great confidence.

January

2008

1 TUESDAY
Moon Age Day 23   Moon Sign Libra

Broadening your horizons in a social sense should begin immediately the year does and it is clear that you presently have what it takes to get on with all sorts of different and potentially useful people. There is no need for Taurean shyness at the moment, so why not begin the year as you would wish to carry on?

2 WEDNESDAY
Moon Age Day 24   Moon Sign Libra

You may still have plenty of energy, but would be wise to tie up a few loose ends today. By tomorrow the Moon enters the zodiac sign of Scorpio. This will bring the lunar low, that period each month when you are regenerating rather than progressing. For now, get on with jobs that simply can't wait until the other end of the week.

3 THURSDAY
Moon Age Day 25   Moon Sign Scorpio

If you reacted properly yesterday you should now find yourself with a little clear space in which to stop and think. Yours is the sort of zodiac sign that responds rather positively to quiet spells and the next couple of days offer you the chance to look forward and plan. You can persuade others to take the strain in the meantime.

4 FRIDAY
Moon Age Day 26   Moon Sign Scorpio

Don't be too quick to take on new responsibilities at the moment – not because you are unequal to them but rather because there may be easier and better ways forward that you can't see at present. A day to get in touch with friends you don't see too often and spend some time in the company of those you know well and love.

73

5 SATURDAY   *Moon Age Day 27   Moon Sign Sagittarius*

The Moon moves on and the weekend offers better prospects for most Taurus subjects. If you have the chance you might decide to take a little trip and to see things that really interest you. The cultural side of your nature is now on show and so anything artistic or historical would probably have a distinct appeal for you.

6 SUNDAY   *Moon Age Day 28   Moon Sign Sagittarius*

Finances would now benefit from a great deal of thought and organisation. It would presently be a mistake to spend large amounts without mulling things over first and making enquiries in order to see if you can get a better bargain elsewhere. A little spring-clean may also be in order if you feel surrounded by clutter.

7 MONDAY   *Moon Age Day 29   Moon Sign Sagittarius*

The Moon in your solar ninth house comes as a definite influence to allow you to get out there in the social mainstream, doing your own thing and making a good impression on others. Taurus is presently accommodating, charming and in every way suited to any sort of company that life throws in your path.

8 TUESDAY   *Moon Age Day 0   Moon Sign Capricorn*

This would be a particularly good time to get rid of old attachments that are no longer any use to you. This trend does not really relate to people but rather 'things'. Taurus is inclined to collect together all sorts of trappings that really only slow you down in the end. A tidier and leaner sort of life would suit you better for 2008.

9 WEDNESDAY   *Moon Age Day 1   Moon Sign Capricorn*

A phase of heightened intuition is on offer and as the Sun passes through your solar ninth house it should become clear that your gut reactions are reliable and have the potential to see you prospering if you take notice of them. Don't worry as much as you might have done recently about family members. Chances are they will be fine.

10 THURSDAY   *Moon Age Day 2   Moon Sign Aquarius*

Material issues can be both difficult to deal with and rather expensive under present trends. If you stop and think about things you should soon realise that the most important gifts in your life at the moment don't cost you anything at all. You can persuade friends to come good for you when it matters the most.

11 FRIDAY   *Moon Age Day 3   Moon Sign Aquarius*

Today should be favourable for intimate relationships and for pushing forward progressively in romantic attachments. Even if you are still working hard in a practical sense, it is the deeper qualities of your nature that predominate. Letting someone know how you really feel about them should be quite easy.

12 SATURDAY   *Moon Age Day 4   Moon Sign Pisces*

There is probably no inherent fear at the moment when it comes to taking quite significant risks. This is particularly true if you are sure of yourself and also of other people, all of whom inspire you with greater confidence. The chances of you being let down around now are quite small, so you can probably afford to be confident.

13 SUNDAY   *Moon Age Day 5   Moon Sign Pisces*

You might be so preoccupied with personal or emotional issues right now that social possibilities are missed. If your partner is quiet or family members are reacting in a rather strange way, you can afford to give them space and time. Meanwhile you can mix with friends who make less demand on you. A light and breezy attitude now works best.

14 MONDAY   *Moon Age Day 6   Moon Sign Pisces*

Present trends encourage you to react very favourably to the input of someone whose ideas and opinions you favour greatly. You show a great desire for freedom and a need to understand not only what is going on around you, but why. You might put love on the back burner as you maintain a more superficial stance.

15 TUESDAY   *Moon Age Day 7   Moon Sign Aries*

This is not a time to be weighed down by mundane issues, but a period during which you need to ring the changes as much as possible. You tend to graze the meadows of life at present rather than worrying yourself about what makes the grass grow. Such interludes are important to a zodiac sign that is usually a natural worrier.

16 WEDNESDAY   *Moon Age Day 8   Moon Sign Aries*

There are small gains to be made today, though you might also be rather contemplative. The Moon is now passing through your solar twelfth house, which always happens just before it returns to your own zodiac sign. This would be an ideal day to get things organised, ahead of a big push that you can start early tomorrow morning.

17 THURSDAY   *Moon Age Day 9   Moon Sign Taurus*

This is the first day of your lunar high – that time each month when the Moon returns to your own zodiac sign. You can afford to push your luck somewhat and should notice that most of your efforts work out well, even though you may not be aware that you are trying very hard. Confidence could well remain generally high until the weekend.

18 FRIDAY   *Moon Age Day 10   Moon Sign Taurus*

This is an ideal time to set out on a few new projects that have been at the back of your mind for a while. Getting others to do your bidding is within your abilities, and there should be no lack of positive indications that you are going in the right direction. In a social sense you can ensure the weekend starts this evening.

19 SATURDAY   *Moon Age Day 11   Moon Sign Gemini*

You have scope to be on the up and up as far as professional matters are concerned, though this might not seem to be particularly important at the weekend. At the same time you show a great need for change and diversity and should have little trouble making the best of impressions wherever you choose to put yourself.

20 SUNDAY
Moon Age Day 12   Moon Sign Gemini

You thrive on doing several different tasks at the same time under present planetary trends and shouldn't have too much difficulty making sure that they are all done well. Sunday could offer new opportunities as far as your love life is concerned and you have what it takes to utter the right words of love that will have someone special melting.

21 MONDAY
Moon Age Day 13   Moon Sign Cancer

It looks as though you might just underestimate your present strengths, and that would be a shame. You are far stronger than you realise, both physically and mentally, and you have such a good attitude to life at present that you can achieve almost anything. All that is required is greater self-belief, together with a little timely help.

22 TUESDAY
Moon Age Day 14   Moon Sign Cancer

You can benefit from the personal side of your life much more at the moment than from practical issues. There is time to talk and an ability on your part to understand the deepest and most intimate responses of those around you. Looking at the natures of other people is presently like gazing through crystal-clear water for you.

23 WEDNESDAY
Moon Age Day 15   Moon Sign Leo

You can now afford to be much more goal-oriented than would often be the case for a Taurus subject. Your organisational skills are second to none and you have what it takes to move mountains in order to achieve your objectives. For all this you can thank the Sun, which now occupies your solar tenth house.

24 THURSDAY
Moon Age Day 16   Moon Sign Leo

If there are conflicts of interest around at the moment, it won't be at all easy to get what you personally want from life, whilst at the same time fulfilling what you see as your obligations towards others. Be careful when making new investments because something that looks like a real bargain could turn out to be anything but.

25 FRIDAY · *Moon Age Day 17 · Moon Sign Virgo*

Trends suggest that leisure rules as the weekend approaches and you could be quite bored with both routines and work issues. It's time to ring the changes and to concentrate on issues that are of no practical use but which interest you all the same. If your time is your own, you could do worse than to take a trip to a romantic setting.

26 SATURDAY · *Moon Age Day 18 · Moon Sign Virgo*

Don't be afraid to travel to new and previously unexplored places this weekend and do everything you can to stimulate the deeper side of your nature. You are intelligent and shrewd but somewhat lacking in stimulation at the moment. The gains you can make are clearly inspired by your own attitude and the arrangements you make now.

27 SUNDAY · *Moon Age Day 19 · Moon Sign Libra*

In a career sense you can have a significant part to play in your own success, though not by actually doing anything today. Rather you should be thinking ahead, planning and determining what attitude and actions to adopt in the days ahead. There is still scope and a great need for personal satisfaction that has nothing to do with practicalities.

28 MONDAY · *Moon Age Day 20 · Moon Sign Libra*

The potential winning streak clearly continues now that little Mercury, as well as the Sun, is in your solar tenth house. This is a working week that should respond positively to your present frame of mind and a time during which you have everything you need to make a good impression when it matters the most. Money matters are well starred.

29 TUESDAY ☿ · *Moon Age Day 21 · Moon Sign Libra*

You can afford to stay generally positive, but watch out because before today is out the Moon returns to your opposite zodiac sign of Scorpio. This can take the wind out of your sails and make some of your plans seem irrelevant or without substance. You need to learn the difference between real visions and mirages.

30 WEDNESDAY ☿ *Moon Age Day 22* *Moon Sign Scorpio*

This is probably not your luckiest period of the month, and you may not be overflowing with energy and confidence. It would be best to allow others to take the strain, whilst you concentrate on thinking up your moves for the future. Despite the lunar low you can be quite content if you only adopt the right attitude.

31 THURSDAY ☿ *Moon Age Day 23* *Moon Sign Scorpio*

If routines become quite stifling, why not take a break from them? There are plenty of people around who can be persuaded to help you out and you have what it takes to show a very positive face to the world at large. By the end of today you can make sure that everything looks much clearer.

February 2008

1 FRIDAY
♀ *Moon Age Day 24   Moon Sign Sagittarius*

The first day of February offers a look at new prospects and an ability to break down certain barriers that have been obvious for the last couple of days. You can now speed towards your longed-for objectives, even if it seems that one or two people are doing all they can to hold you back. The best response to difficulties now is to laugh.

2 SATURDAY
♀ *Moon Age Day 25   Moon Sign Sagittarius*

If you make sure you can get out and about today you could meet people who will be of real use to you in the future, as well as individuals who simply interest you. Concentrating on the same old things is not to be recommended at this time, and you will be far better off taking a fairly superficial attitude when possible.

3 SUNDAY
♀ *Moon Age Day 26   Moon Sign Sagittarius*

Brief vacations and intellectual pursuits suit you well and there are some gains to be made as a result of simply looking at old situations in new and revolutionary ways. You are able to move close to the end of a particular phase in your life, and should be fortunate in any dealings with loved ones, as well as the world at large.

4 MONDAY
♀ *Moon Age Day 27   Moon Sign Capricorn*

There is a strongly competitive element about Taurus at the moment and it is clear that you needn't give in on anything once you have set your mind to it. If there are individuals around who are just as anxious to win as you are, it looks as though the scene could be set for some interesting and rewarding competitions!

5 TUESDAY ☿ *Moon Age Day 28 Moon Sign Capricorn*

You can make this a forward-looking period in a professional sense. There may well be offers on the table that you would not want to turn down, but at the same time you might be spoiled for choice. Decisions will have to be made and if you can't work things out for yourself, it's worth turning to a good friend or colleague for advice.

6 WEDNESDAY ☿ *Moon Age Day 0 Moon Sign Aquarius*

Motivation is clearly the key to success at the moment, which is why you won't get a lot done if you keep taking on jobs you hate. Even if unsavoury things do have to be done, these should be shared out fairly and there is no reason why you should always be at the front of the queue. The time is right to prompt someone else into taking a turn.

7 THURSDAY ☿ *Moon Age Day 1 Moon Sign Aquarius*

This could prove to be a slightly more testing day in a professional sense, though it should be an easier time for those who are between jobs or retired. If your time is your own this would be a good day to try something completely new. Even if you don't have very much money at present you remain, as always, very resourceful.

8 FRIDAY ☿ *Moon Age Day 2 Moon Sign Aquarius*

With the Moon now in your solar eleventh house you have scope today to take a few hours to yourself and to do something that is of no importance whatsoever, but which suits you personally. Why not take a friend along for the ride and seek out a little excitement? What form this takes depends on your present fancy.

9 SATURDAY ☿ *Moon Age Day 3 Moon Sign Pisces*

Now is the time to widen your horizons and to make this a weekend to remember. There are plenty of people around who can be persuaded to join in the fun. When Taurus is on form you can be the most charming and entertaining company around and you certainly can show yourself to be energetic under present planetary trends.

10 SUNDAY ☿   *Moon Age Day 4   Moon Sign Pisces*

You can now afford to take a tough and uncompromising stance if it proves to be necessary. This fact could shock anyone who believes you to be a pushover, but the fact is that Taurus can be one of the most stubborn of all the zodiac signs. At least some of your time now could be spent supporting someone who is having their own problems.

11 MONDAY ☿   *Moon Age Day 5   Moon Sign Aries*

Along comes a professional boost and you can make this the most rewarding week of the month in the job stakes. But although you are active and enterprising, for the next couple of days you are also capable of being very contemplative. Your mindset represents a formidable combination, as the world is about to learn!

12 TUESDAY ☿   *Moon Age Day 6   Moon Sign Aries*

Routines are not for you at any stage during this week, which is why you may well decide to ring the changes and to get some variety into your life. There are still moments during which you can look deep inside yourself, but these represent only short interludes, encouraged by a twelfth-house Moon.

13 WEDNESDAY ☿   *Moon Age Day 7   Moon Sign Taurus*

Today the green light is on for you as the Moon returns to your own zodiac sign of Taurus. The time is right to take all the initiative you have and make it work for you, particularly in professional and practical matters. Even apparent disadvantages can be turned in your favour, and you can persuade plenty of people to lend a hand.

14 THURSDAY ☿   *Moon Age Day 8   Moon Sign Taurus*

This is another excellent period for professional developments but you needn't be concentrating exclusively on the practical aspects of life. Taurus has a chance to have fun and to display more physical energy than has probably been the case for a number of weeks. Comfort and security may well be far from the front of your mind now.

15 FRIDAY   ☿   *Moon Age Day 9*   *Moon Sign Gemini*

This would be a great time to travel, and although the weather still won't be up to much as far as Britain is concerned, there is a great big world out there that Taurus loves to explore. However, if foreign shores are impossible at the moment, be prepared to find somewhere to go that at least feels like being in the sunshine.

16 SATURDAY   ☿   *Moon Age Day 10*   *Moon Sign Gemini*

If you have to deal with authority figures you could not pick a better time to do so than right now. You will also be in a very good position to formalise long-term commitments and to sign up partnerships of some sort that are really going to work on your behalf in the months and even the years ahead.

17 SUNDAY   ☿   *Moon Age Day 11*   *Moon Sign Cancer*

There should be little to stand in your way in most respects, and with the Moon now in your solar third house it looks as though you have scope to express your emotions rather better than might sometimes be the case. This is especially important in personal attachments and you can offer great reassurance to your partner.

18 MONDAY   ☿   *Moon Age Day 12*   *Moon Sign Cancer*

Career satisfaction can be achieved through being well organised and by getting others to work along lines you know to be sensible and productive. Trends stimulate good powers of persuasion and a very positive psychological approach that seems to be infectious. Not everyone may be on your side now but most should be when it really matters.

19 TUESDAY   ☿   *Moon Age Day 13*   *Moon Sign Leo*

You have to be prepared to work very hard under present trends but the results should make all your efforts more than worthwhile. Nobody can pitch in better than Taurus and when you know you are on a winning streak you can put in far more effort than almost any other individual. Now you can push on simply because you wish to.

20 WEDNESDAY
Moon Age Day 14   Moon Sign Leo

Trends suggest that family matters could be high on your list of priorities around this time. Maybe family members are demanding your attention, or it could be that you are supporting someone who is going through a difficult period. Whatever you are doing, your strength lies in a cheerful attitude and a sense of humour that is infectious.

21 THURSDAY
Moon Age Day 15   Moon Sign Leo

Now is the time to be frugal with your purchases and if possible avoid spending too much money. It isn't that you are going to make yourself poor by doing so, simply that you may be in line for some better bargains in a few days. In any case the things that are most important to you at the moment should cost you nothing at all.

22 FRIDAY
Moon Age Day 16   Moon Sign Virgo

The Moon now in your solar fifth house assists you with exciting changes to your romantic life. If you are in a settled relationship this will show itself in the form of a more progressive attachment. Taureans who are looking for a new love should focus all their attention on people who are coming along at any time now.

23 SATURDAY
Moon Age Day 17   Moon Sign Virgo

You can persuade friends to be both supportive and stimulating at this time and to offer you the chance to relax a little, whilst they take some of the strain in potentially difficult situations. Life can be a breeze for those of you who are willing to take a back seat, but of course Taurus hates to let go of the reins and this can be a slight problem.

24 SUNDAY
Moon Age Day 18   Moon Sign Libra

The positive aspects of life should stand out very significantly at the moment, even if people you mix with are having a slightly more difficult time than you are. This is likely to be a day during which you are willing to count your blessings. Don't be too quick to take on anything new for now, and think carefully before making decisions.

25 MONDAY *Moon Age Day 19 Moon Sign Libra*

Venus is now in your solar tenth house, and one aspect of its presence there is to stimulate contact with people who can be of great use to you in a practical sense. You have scope to be at the forefront of any new activity that is presently invading your social circle, and you are well able to impress others with your very varied talents.

26 TUESDAY *Moon Age Day 20 Moon Sign Scorpio*

Unless you are working particularly hard now the arrival of the lunar low might go quite unnoticed. It's possible that you will be slightly quieter than has been the case recently but you remain basically optimistic and anxious to enjoy yourself whenever possible. What you shouldn't do today is make important decisions for the future.

27 WEDNESDAY *Moon Age Day 21 Moon Sign Scorpio*

Things can go slightly wrong in a personal sense, which is why you might decide to keep a generally low profile for today and tomorrow. It isn't that you are creating problems for yourself, merely that life doesn't seem to favour the actions you take or the things you say. The world at large seems to be oversensitive now.

28 THURSDAY *Moon Age Day 22 Moon Sign Scorpio*

If you can put yourself in the midst of a group of people who inspire you, today can be quite enterprising. However, the lunar low is still around and you might be better off watching and waiting for a few hours. All that glistens is not gold, and though you realise this fact most of the time you could be somewhat blind to it now.

29 FRIDAY *Moon Age Day 23 Moon Sign Sagittarius*

When it comes to practical efforts you can get by with a combination of common sense and intuition. You have scope to speed things up somewhat at the end of this working week and to get back to the generally progressive attitude you have had through most of February. Someone could surprise you with a change of attitude.

⑧ March

2008

1 SATURDAY — Moon Age Day 24 — Moon Sign Sagittarius

A day to establish contact with influential or very inspiring people, and don't worry if their attitude seems to be very infectious. Much of your effort today can be ploughed into a specific furrow and you shouldn't have any trouble persuading others that your point of view is both valid and worthwhile. This is Taurus at its best.

2 SUNDAY — Moon Age Day 25 — Moon Sign Capricorn

You now have the chance to apply your imaginative ideas to practical situations, and once again you will be in a very good position to feather your own nest. At the same time you can assist any friend who has not been so lucky of late, and as always you can show that innate sensitivity that definitely sets your zodiac aside from the mainstream.

3 MONDAY — Moon Age Day 26 — Moon Sign Capricorn

You should be able to put yourself in an idealistic frame of mind at the start of this week and needn't take no for an answer when it comes to achieving some of your most longed-for objectives for the sake of other people. Your generosity knows no bounds, and you can show yourself to be inspirational in your approach to those around you.

4 TUESDAY — Moon Age Day 27 — Moon Sign Capricorn

A day to look ahead carefully before embarking on any new venture. Beware of signing important documents without reading small print carefully and, if necessary, getting some specialist advice. It is around this time that you could discover you are in possession of something that is rather more valuable than you thought.

5 WEDNESDAY   *Moon Age Day 28   Moon Sign Aquarius*

The impact that others have on you could be quite strong at this time, and you have scope to make the most favourable impression imaginable. This is not to suggest that everyone takes to you and there might be people who are difficult to deal with. One area of life you can get to work really well for you at present is romance.

6 THURSDAY   *Moon Age Day 29   Moon Sign Aquarius*

There are signs that you now tend to enjoy working with others more than you do in a solo capacity. This isn't always the case because Taurus is quite capable of working alone. What probably attracts you the most about co-operation at present is the chance to pool ideas and to reach far more lucrative and even enjoyable conclusions as a result.

7 FRIDAY   *Moon Age Day 0   Moon Sign Pisces*

Even if you are very fast-thinking yourself at the moment, it's possible that other people might be much slower on the uptake. This could prove to be rather frustrating and your best response is to display that important Taurean patience in order to deal with the situation. Friends could prove themselves to be loyal.

8 SATURDAY   *Moon Age Day 1   Moon Sign Pisces*

Trends indicate that many of your most important decisions at the moment are influenced by the people entering your life. You have a great capacity for love and show the fact at every turn. Taurus is at its most affectionate and this ought to be the sort of weekend during which you spread your own particular brand of joy far and wide.

9 SUNDAY   *Moon Age Day 2   Moon Sign Aries*

Another good day is possible, and can also be a time during which positive actions on your part can save you a great deal of time later. You would be wise to stay away from anything tedious or boring and, if possible, get out into the good fresh air. The first stirrings of spring are at hand and Taurus appreciates the fact better than anyone.

10 MONDAY
Moon Age Day 3   Moon Sign Aries

You need to sit back and take a look at life in a somewhat different way today and you have the time to do so. The Moon is in your solar twelfth house and that encourages you to be rather more contemplative and less inclined to rush around. There will not be a better opportunity to be alone with your thoughts than this one.

11 TUESDAY
Moon Age Day 4   Moon Sign Taurus

The lunar high returns and brings with it the potential for a sudden surge in energy and a great desire to get things done. New projects are in store and you have what it takes to break down barriers from the past in order to get what you want from life. Bringing others round to your point of view should be child's play under present astrological trends.

12 WEDNESDAY
Moon Age Day 5   Moon Sign Taurus

A day to get an early start and pitch into important tasks. You are half-way towards anything at all whilst the Moon occupies your zodiac sign and will show yourself to be willing to work long and hard to achieve your objectives. Somehow you should also find the time today to enjoy yourself and to entertain those around you.

13 THURSDAY
Moon Age Day 6   Moon Sign Gemini

There is the possibility of a few conflicts today. These might come about because of the attitude of colleagues or friends, or because you are in such a forceful frame of mind yourself. On specific occasions it can be like an irresistible force meeting and irremovable object – and there is nobody more stubborn than Taurus.

14 FRIDAY
Moon Age Day 7   Moon Sign Gemini

A new and more beneficial phase with regard to money can now be spurred off by the Moon entering your solar second house. There it assists other planetary positions to offer you greater control of your resources. You may not be much better off overall, but you could be managing what you have much more effectively.

15 SATURDAY
Moon Age Day 8   Moon Sign Cancer

There are new friendships on the way, or at least the possibility of them, and you are about as sociable now as you will be during March. Spring is showing itself more every day and that should suit you fine because you are a spring-born individual yourself. Your strength lies in being generally cheerful and finding ways to lift the spirits of friends.

16 SUNDAY
Moon Age Day 9   Moon Sign Cancer

A somewhat assertive and even argumentative attitude to life may be apparent now, and since this is encouraged by Mars, a fairly slow-moving planet, it is a phase that could be around for a while. This trend is only likely to show itself in situations where other people are trying to put one over on you – or at least when you think they are!

17 MONDAY
Moon Age Day 10   Moon Sign Cancer

This is a great time for getting together with like-minded individuals, and a day when you may decide to leave less favoured colleagues or acquaintances very much alone. There is a focus on making new friends at this time, probably as a result of initiatives that are coming into your life through a change of attitude.

18 TUESDAY
Moon Age Day 11   Moon Sign Leo

A good time to relate to others intellectually and a period during which you can learn from them about subjects that have been at the back of your mind. Being willing to change your mind is important, and you can allow some of the intransigence of Taurus to take a holiday for the moment. The more flexible you are, the greater your potential.

19 WEDNESDAY
Moon Age Day 12   Moon Sign Leo

If it seems impossible to please everyone today, your best response is not to try to do so. Better by far to concentrate on one or two specific individuals – the sort of people who respond well to your personality for most of the time. Romance is looking good, especially for Taureans who are now actively looking for love.

20 THURSDAY *Moon Age Day 13   Moon Sign Virg*

You should be in your element today if you get yourself involved in heady debates or in situations that demand you think quickly. Intuitive and perceptive, you are able to twist and turn with the subject matter at hand and won't lose any chance to 'say it how it is'. Whether others will agree remains to be seen.

21 FRIDAY *Moon Age Day 14   Moon Sign Virg*

Mercury entering your solar eleventh house now offers possible changes to your social life. A breath of fresh air comes along and most of it is responsive to the point of view of those you mix with regularly. Any tendency towards change should be grabbed by you with both hands, and you needn't be afraid to break old habits.

22 SATURDAY *Moon Age Day 15   Moon Sign Libr*

If your thoughts and moods fluctuate somewhat this weekend, you may discover that you are able to overcome past problems simply by looking at them in a new and revolutionary way. A break from the ordinary is favoured in your social and personal life too. The more you surprise others, the greater your personal satisfaction will be.

23 SUNDAY *Moon Age Day 16   Moon Sign Libr*

Trends hint at there being a few obstacles to get over or round today, though these are more likely to be restricted to work, so if your time is your own this is less likely to be an obvious trend. Socially you can be on top form and might well shelve jobs you don't want to do in favour of enjoying yourself. Travel would be good right now.

24 MONDAY *Moon Age Day 17   Moon Sign Libr*

Even if committing yourself to the task at hand is easy, there is just a possibility that you will need to work hard to maintain a high level of concentration as the day wears on. Later the Moon enters Scorpio and from that position it doesn't really do you many material favours. A quiet evening would probably suit you best.

25 TUESDAY   *Moon Age Day 18   Moon Sign Scorpio*

This is an ideal time to slow down and to take a break. The lunar low does nothing to help you to be progressive, either in your attitude or in terms of practical moves. It would be better by far at the moment to watch and wait, whilst at the same time taking a few hours to yourself in order to contemplate in the way only Taurus can.

26 WEDNESDAY   *Moon Age Day 19   Moon Sign Scorpio*

Your physical vitality may not be great, but that doesn't mean you need to be unhappy. It's simply a case of going with the flow and treading water more than you usually would. Instead of trying to make everything work out the way you want, why not watch for a while? Some things will come good of their own accord.

27 THURSDAY   *Moon Age Day 20   Moon Sign Sagittarius*

Though you now have scope to be more positive in your attitude, you might feel that you have to please too many people and that you would rather simply do what suits you. There is nothing wrong with feeling this way except for the fact that you have a very active conscience and might feel guilty if you feel you have been selfish.

28 FRIDAY   *Moon Age Day 21   Moon Sign Sagittarius*

Today responds best if you keep up a busy schedule and get stuck into practical matters. With the weekend in view you might also be planning social events and maybe enjoyable outings. In almost every sense you are now able to look ahead and see the future much more clearly than has been the case for a few weeks.

29 SATURDAY   *Moon Age Day 22   Moon Sign Sagittarius*

Learning to relax and to be content with your lot is your homework for this weekend. You needn't get anxious, particularly about situations you cannot possibly alter. If you do get a little depressed by anything, it's worth casting your gaze towards those who have much greater problems but who are dealing with them cheerfully and well.

30 SUNDAY · *Moon Age Day 23 · Moon Sign Capricor*

If you can seek out some freedom-loving individuals today that
good because such people can help you to broaden your ow
horizons. Attitude is very important when you are approachin
anything new, and if you believe in yourself there is very little tha
you cannot achieve. You can make every situation today a learnin
experience.

31 MONDAY · *Moon Age Day 24 · Moon Sign Capricor*

Enjoying yourself ought to be fairly easy on the last day of March
especially if you can get others to draw you into their own littl
adventures. Even if you are not doing anything too outrageous a
the moment, you know how to contribute and can show yourself t
be more co-operative than ever.

April

2008

TUESDAY   *Moon Age Day 25   Moon Sign Aquarius*

With Venus so strong in your solar eleventh house you will be no April Fool, and can enjoy any sort of social gathering to the full. Personal attachments could also bring a greater sense of joy and you have what it takes to turn heads, even outside of your normal social circle. Money matters take on a new perspective now.

WEDNESDAY   *Moon Age Day 26   Moon Sign Aquarius*

Now is the time to think less about what you can take from either friendships or associations with colleagues and rather mull over what you can offer. It's a definite fact of life at the moment that the more you give, the greater can be your own satisfaction and success. You can turn new social encounters into important friendships at this time.

THURSDAY   *Moon Age Day 27   Moon Sign Pisces*

Your personal behaviour can be influenced now by other-worldly, intuitive and even psychic perceptions. Hunches could prove to be very reliable and you shouldn't have to work hard in order to increase the level of your general luck. Best of all you should know instinctively how other people are thinking and how they will behave.

FRIDAY   *Moon Age Day 28   Moon Sign Pisces*

The Sun occupies your solar twelfth house throughout the first two-thirds of April and makes this a period for letting go of outmoded thinking patterns and material items you no longer use or need. As a result a great spring-clean is called for – both inside and outside of your mind. You can make this a joyful experience.

5 SATURDAY · *Moon Age Day 29   Moon Sign Pisc*

You have scope to show yourself to be a giving person this weeken
particularly if most of what you do is undertaken for those aroun
you. It's a funny thing but the more you offer, the greater are th
gifts that come your way. No zodiac sign typifies this more tha
yours. Socially speaking you can be great fun to have aroun
throughout today.

6 SUNDAY *Moon Age Day 0   Moon Sign Ar*

Success is on offer if you go with the flow more than has sometim
been the case across the last week or two. With changi
astrological patterns, this becomes more likely. However there
just a chance that you will indulge in woolly thinking on occasio
when a very decisive and direct attitude would be more helpful.

7 MONDAY *Moon Age Day 1   Moon Sign Ar*

If there are issues to deal with today, these ought to be sorted o
ahead of the lunar high that comes along tomorrow. You shouldr
mind a little routine for the moment and have what it takes to so
out situations, even if to others they look like a tangled ball
string. Patience is one of your best virtues, and you can make su
it shows now.

8 TUESDAY *Moon Age Day 2   Moon Sign Taur*

Self-confidence and a simple faith in your own abilities are all y
need to make a success of today. With the lunar high on your sid
don't be surprised if Lady Luck pays a visit to your life, though
has to be said that in the main you make your own luck at preser
Above all now you can afford to be very idealistic.

9 WEDNESDAY *Moon Age Day 3   Moon Sign Taur*

This is a time when you should be looking at far-reaching plans a
working out how to make them work much earlier than you mig
previously have expected. Trends assist you to remain ve
optimistic, to know what you want from life and to get the peop
on board who will be in the best possible position to help you ot

10 THURSDAY   *Moon Age Day 4   Moon Sign Gemini*

There probably isn't much doubt about you being outspoken today - in fact there are times when you might be better to bite your tongue. Such situations usually come about when Taurus is defending someone else, and that could well be the scenario now. It's worth making certain you know your facts before really having a go at anyone.

11 FRIDAY   *Moon Age Day 5   Moon Sign Gemini*

When it comes to personal attachments you may not be going through the best period you are likely to experience either this month or even this year. Venus is now in your solar twelfth house and this can sometimes make attachments look less than sparkling. Much depends on your own attitude and the effort you put in personally.

12 SATURDAY   *Moon Age Day 6   Moon Sign Cancer*

Around this time you should be taking time off from ordinary routines so that you can find moments for deep insights into life as a whole and where it is presently leading you. A few minor alterations might be necessary, and though these may not seem like much they can have a tremendous bearing on your longer-term future.

13 SUNDAY   *Moon Age Day 7   Moon Sign Cancer*

It might be necessary to weigh the balance between work and home around now, so if you have some time to yourself on this Sunday, don't be afraid to take a few moments to be on your own and to think. There might be distractions about, but these needn't prevent you from finding a little corner where you can meditate in peace.

14 MONDAY   *Moon Age Day 8   Moon Sign Leo*

There are signs that it isn't what it is going on in front of your face that you find so appealing today but rather what is happening behind the scenes. It's clear that if your curiosity is aroused, you will not stop moving stones just to see what is under them. Just be careful that you don't annoy anyone else by appearing to be nosey.

15 TUESDAY
Moon Age Day 9   Moon Sign Le

This is hardly the best time of the month during which to be relying heavily on other people. In the main your interests are best served by going it alone, especially when it comes to projects that are dear to your heart. Taking on additional responsibilities shouldn't bother you in the slightest – just as long as you are left to get on with things.

16 WEDNESDAY
Moon Age Day 10   Moon Sign Virg

The Moon now in your solar fifth house helps you to reach a stage when you want to concentrate on personal fulfilment. You usually do a great deal to support those around you but there are times when it is necessary to look solely at your own needs – if only for a hour or two. Don't feel guilty as a result.

17 THURSDAY
Moon Age Day 11   Moon Sign Virg

A day to relax and trust that most matters will turn out well in the long run. This is not a time to exhibit undue anxiety, if only because you might telegraph the fact to others and make them worry too. In any case most of what you are anxious about either is unimportant or can be dispelled like the morning mist.

18 FRIDAY
Moon Age Day 12   Moon Sign Libr.

Trends suggest that personal recognition isn't too important to you today. What matters more is making certain that things are done efficiently and properly. It might well be easy to become annoyed with individuals who won't do what you tell them, or people who seem determined to throw a spanner in the works simply to be mischievous.

19 SATURDAY
Moon Age Day 13   Moon Sign Libr.

Mental talents and the ability to communicate your ideas and opinions to others are definitely strong at the moment. You can make this a crackerjack of a weekend and particularly so in a social sense. All the more reason to avoid getting tied down too much with domestic responsibilities and to do your best to mix as much as possible.

20 SUNDAY *Moon Age Day 14   Moon Sign Libra*

Be prepared to keep up the pace and get what you want from today because tomorrow and Tuesday might be quieter and less eventful generally. Although you may not end today one penny better off than you started it, you will still be in the market for significant gains. However, these are all more likely to be personal rather than material.

21 MONDAY *Moon Age Day 15   Moon Sign Scorpio*

The Moon now moves into Scorpio, bringing the lunar low for you and one of the quieter interludes of the month. There probably isn't really much point in knocking your head against a wall because it will be difficult to get everything you want today. It would be better by far to watch and wait, whilst you plan in detail for what lies ahead of you.

22 TUESDAY *Moon Age Day 16   Moon Sign Scorpio*

Many issues could be resolved at this time – if you could only summon up the energy to think about them! Things are the way they are for the moment, and you could well become frustrated if you try to alter anything significant right now. By tomorrow you can be much more dynamic, but for the moment your best option is to relax and float.

23 WEDNESDAY *Moon Age Day 17   Moon Sign Sagittarius*

Now is the time to apply a little self-discipline, and in your dealings with others it is important to sort out the wheat from the chaff. In a practical sense you should only throw in your lot with those who have proven themselves to be reliable and capable. Co-operation is very important now, but so is careful selection before you commit yourself.

24 THURSDAY *Moon Age Day 18   Moon Sign Sagittarius*

The planetary focus remains specifically on personal interests and abilities. It might seem selfish, but it isn't. Unless you get things running the way you know they should, you won't have either the time or the money to share with those you love. There are times when Taurus is very practical indeed, and this is such a period.

25 FRIDAY
Moon Age Day 19   Moon Sign Sagittarius

It could be that you feel like getting away from routines today, though it's more likely you will be planning a break for the weekend. Remaining busy is fine, but it will be very easy to grow bored with routines and to tinker with things as a result. This can be quite entertaining, but could lead to a few problems.

26 SATURDAY
Moon Age Day 20   Moon Sign Capricorn

Communication is to the fore as Saturday dawns, offering a chance to talk freely to just about anyone you come across now. You might decide to go on a shopping spree, or even to have a trip out with your partner or a friend. What wouldn't be too good today would be to stick around usual places, doing the same old things.

27 SUNDAY
Moon Age Day 21   Moon Sign Capricorn

There are signs that personal relationships won't be doing you too many favours today, which is why it's worth sticking to friendships and opting for a light and superficial view of life. By tomorrow you can once again be committed to looking at romance or deep commitment, but that is simply not the best approach at the moment.

28 MONDAY
Moon Age Day 22   Moon Sign Aquarius

Your professional life is highlighted today, prompting you to concentrate very hard in order to get things right. Others could well be offering timely assistance, but the more so if you are willing to ask for help. Sometimes Taurus can be too proud for its own good. It's worth calling in a few favours – you shouldn't be refused.

29 TUESDAY
Moon Age Day 23   Moon Sign Aquarius

The Sun is now firmly in your solar first house and its position there accentuates your need to do your own thing. Personal freedom becomes more and more important and you probably won't take at all kindly to being held back by anyone. Some Taureans might be thinking about a change of job at this time or maybe a house move.

30 WEDNESDAY   *Moon Age Day 24   Moon Sign Aquarius*

You can make this one of the most rewarding periods of the month in a social sense, so just as April is departing, the focus is firmly on enjoyment with friends. Work might seem to be getting in the way, but there are opportunities for you to mix business with pleasure. It's simply a case of thinking things through.

May
2008

1 THURSDAY
Moon Age Day 25   Moon Sign Pisces

Venus enters your solar first house at last, and this should be a very pleasing development. Personal attachments might have been a bit odd whilst Venus was in your solar twelfth house, but now things can be made more settled in the romantic stakes. The kind and loving side of Taurus should now be on display much more.

2 FRIDAY
Moon Age Day 26   Moon Sign Pisces

For a couple of days the Moon will be passing through your solar twelfth house. Taken together with other planetary positions this encourages a fairly dreamy phase and a period during which you may be less inclined to push yourself. Your intuition will be much heightened, and you can make sure you are fascinating to others.

3 SATURDAY
Moon Age Day 27   Moon Sign Aries

It ought to be a piece of cake getting relatives and friends to do things for you at the moment. Such are your powers of persuasion that you could sell fridges to Eskimos. When it comes to financial matters it might be best to defer to someone who has more experience of a very particular situation than you do yourself.

4 SUNDAY
Moon Age Day 28   Moon Sign Aries

Trends encourage you to remain quieter than usual but to be just a magnetic and attractive to others. You can smoulder with sexiness when in social settings and may even get a little attention you would rather not have at all. Stand by for a sudden acceleration tomorrow, but for the moment simply make the most of your popularity.

5 MONDAY
Moon Age Day 0   Moon Sign Taurus

It's time for you to press ahead with big plans and to make yourself the master of your own destiny to a much greater extent. You shouldn't have any difficulty getting on with anyone you meet, and that's important whilst the lunar high is around. There are so many gains to be made, and all of them are about people in one way or another.

6 TUESDAY
Moon Age Day 1   Moon Sign Taurus

Short-term goals can be dealt with at lightning speed, and longer-term ambitions shouldn't take too much longer. Whilst others are thinking about acting, you can get things sorted. This can be a great advantage because it enables you to push ahead much quicker than either you or almost anyone else thought possible.

7 WEDNESDAY
Moon Age Day 2   Moon Sign Gemini

Although the Moon has now moved into Gemini you can still steal a march on the competition. Now you can do it as much by stealth as by direct action. Be careful though, because you don't want to be accused of duplicity and should be scrupulously open in your dealings. You can afford to let romance light your life later in the day.

8 THURSDAY
Moon Age Day 3   Moon Sign Gemini

Make this a good day for acquiring new ideas and useful input from the direction of others. Whether it is material you gain from direct or indirect sources, there isn't much doubt about your ability to turn everything you hear to your own advantage. An entertaining period is on offer when it comes to younger family members.

9 FRIDAY
Moon Age Day 4   Moon Sign Cancer

Happiness and satisfaction are there for the taking as a result of social engagements and attachments. You have scope to be in the spotlight and shouldn't mind at all if you realise that others have been talking about you. Fortunately most of what they have to say is very positive and you can bask in their compliments.

101

10 SATURDAY   *Moon Age Day 5   Moon Sign Cancer*

You can best avoid tensions at home by speaking your mind, though as diplomatically as you can manage. If you are feeling slightly under the weather you would probably respond well to a breath of fresh air because Taurus is, of necessity, a lover of the outdoors. This will be especially true if you have been cooped up for some days.

11 SUNDAY   *Moon Age Day 6   Moon Sign Leo*

It's worth encouraging better family support all round, and not just for your own sake. Convincing others to pull together is part of what today is about, and you have what it takes to get others to follow your lead. Taurus can be quite contemplative under present trends, but that needn't prevent you from speaking your mind too.

12 MONDAY   *Moon Age Day 7   Moon Sign Leo*

Don't be afraid to be unique in the way you dress and act at the moment. The Sun is strong in your solar first house and that means amongst other things, that you should be quite willing to be an individual. If this enables you to attract the attention of a somewhat surprised world, then so much the better for you.

13 TUESDAY   *Moon Age Day 8   Moon Sign Virgo*

Besides being potentially creative and very affectionate at the moment, you can show yourself to be deeply magnetic and very attractive to most of the people you meet today. Even a slight tendency to be bossy may be no bad thing if it means you can persuade someone to do something that they have been strenuously avoiding.

14 WEDNESDAY   *Moon Age Day 9   Moon Sign Virgo*

Recognition of your own ego is not only important at the moment, it's vital. You have scope to entertain others, and as far as your home is concerned it's likely to be a case of open house. Taurus is in a position to act on impulse to a much greater extent than would normally be the case. Use your present influence at every opportunity.

15 THURSDAY   *Moon Age Day 10   Moon Sign Virgo*

There are signs that domestic and family issues could be taking up a fair percentage of your time, and you show immense consideration for the well-being and general feelings of those around you. You can be quite stubborn if you feel yourself pushed into a corner, but in the main you should be more relaxed than would often seem to be the case.

16 FRIDAY   *Moon Age Day 11   Moon Sign Libra*

Like a true Taurean you need to be quite sure about yourself before embarking on any particular course of action and this trend is especially enhanced under the present influence of the Moon. Your careful attitude can be very important at present and should prevent you from making a dreadful mistake. An ideal time to show tact and diplomacy.

17 SATURDAY   *Moon Age Day 12   Moon Sign Libra*

With Venus now strong in your solar second house you could well be enjoying the fruits of your previous efforts and might be slightly better off than you expected in a financial sense. All the same some care is necessary where money is concerned, particularly if you feel tempted to overspend.

18 SUNDAY   *Moon Age Day 13   Moon Sign Scorpio*

The lunar low need not have too much of a bearing on your general progress this time around. There are strong supporting planetary influences, not least that first-house Sun. Nevertheless you would be well advised to take life fairly steadily and to rest and relax on those occasions when circumstances seem to permit.

19 MONDAY   *Moon Age Day 14   Moon Sign Scorpio*

There could be a few mishaps at work and though this shouldn't be too much of a problem, your ingenuity is not highlighted as much as of late. It might be necessary to look out for the support of someone who is an expert in their field. Calling in favours is not difficult for Taurus because you do so much for others.

20 TUESDAY   *Moon Age Day 15   Moon Sign Scorpi*

Once the Moon moves on, which happens around the middle of the day, you can afford to be up for anything and eager to push ahead. It's time to put yourself about and to show the world at large what you are made of. False modesty is no virtue and you are able to accomplish just about anything your fertile mind can imagine.

21 WEDNESDAY *Moon Age Day 16   Moon Sign Sagittariu*

A day to take some time out to organise things, not only in material sense but with regard to the way your mind is working at present. If you don't, you could be accused of being muddled in your thoughts and competitors can use this fact against you. A few hours out of the social maelstrom will probably appeal to you great deal today.

22 THURSDAY   *Moon Age Day 17   Moon Sign Sagittariu*

New financial beginnings now become entirely possible, and if you make use of your tremendous intuition you are hardly likely to make mistakes when it comes to cash. As always you are careful and astute in your dealings, and can also find time today to show tremendous support for a friend or your partner.

23 FRIDAY   *Moon Age Day 18   Moon Sign Capricorn*

There are different views around at the moment and the period can be quite informative. Taurus is always anxious to learn and that is particularly the case at the moment. Life itself is your schoolroom and you never tire of realising that there is something else to be taken on board. Today has scope to be very entertaining.

24 SATURDAY   *Moon Age Day 19   Moon Sign Capricorn*

It's possible that you won't like the look of certain matters that rise to the surface today. You could get slightly crabby and over concerned with details that are not of the slightest importance in the greater scheme of things. It would be better to be alone on occasion today, rather than flying off the handle.

25 SUNDAY   *Moon Age Day 20   Moon Sign Capricorn*

Venus remains in your solar second house, and is joined there by the Sun. Attracting the more pleasant things from life shouldn't be difficult, and you can certainly show yourself to be refined and highly sociable at the moment. On the other side of the coin you could well begin to hate anything sordid, grubby or lacking in culture.

26 MONDAY   *Moon Age Day 21   Moon Sign Aquarius*

Your judgement is sound in professional matters and you have what it takes to put yourself into the best possible position at work. Taurus subjects who have been thinking about a change of career may be well advised to look around at the moment, and there is also a good chance that you can seek out a new opportunity.

27 TUESDAY   ☿ *Moon Age Day 22   Moon Sign Aquarius*

In a domestic sense you can make this a fairly rewarding period, though finding time to please loved ones as much as you might wish may not be easy. Your time is split between your home and the needs that the greater world has of you. You need to effectively compartmentalise today in order to avoid disappointing everyone.

28 WEDNESDAY ☿   *Moon Age Day 23   Moon Sign Pisces*

It is still difficult for you to be in two places at the same time, though if you co-operate successfully with others you might be able to persuade them to do some of the running around for you. Do what you can to show yourself to be capable and don't hedge your bets when it comes to decisions. It's time to show your mettle.

29 THURSDAY   ☿ *Moon Age Day 24   Moon Sign Pisces*

It would be very easy today to get carried away with money matters. As is often the case for Taurus you can be fascinated by luxury goods and could so easily overspend. This would be a shame, especially as you have what it takes to root out the things you need for a fraction of the apparent cost. Use your ingenuity today.

30 FRIDAY   ☿   *Moon Age Day 25   Moon Sign Aries*

The Moon is now in your solar twelfth house, suggesting that you respond very positively to a little solitude. Don't be pushed into anything that doesn't appeal to you, and rather than making mistakes, make it plain that you need time in order to make the correct judgement. Why not seek out amusing friends?

31 SATURDAY   ☿   *Moon Age Day 26   Moon Sign Aries*

You have scope to get your own way a great deal in practical concerns and can be quite acquisitive under present trends. Once again you need to fight the urge to splurge money on things you don't really need. The result of doing so under present planetary trends is almost certain to be a large amount of buyer's remorse.

June

2008

1 SUNDAY ☿ *Moon Age Day 27* *Moon Sign Taurus*

There won't be a more dynamic start to a month than this during the whole of the year. You should certainly commence June as you mean to go on, and be strongly supportive of anything that takes your fancy. Your mind is now original and you needn't be held back by shadows from the past or fears regarding the future.

2 MONDAY ☿ *Moon Age Day 28* *Moon Sign Taurus*

A day for a few minor triumphs, when you can make sure you are practically everyone's cup of tea. Now is the right time to push for something you really want and the only possible difficulty comes if you continue to spend money you probably don't have on things you really don't need.

3 TUESDAY ☿ *Moon Age Day 29* *Moon Sign Gemini*

Moneymaking ventures might look quite exciting, but you would be well advised to think carefully before embarking. Money is the only area of your life that needs special attention under present trends, and you certainly should not part with cash willy-nilly.

4 WEDNESDAY ☿ *Moon Age Day 0* *Moon Sign Gemini*

You are now in a position to stabilise finance and monetary matters as the Sun strengthens its position in your solar second house. If you need advice you shouldn't go short of it but not everything that is said to you will be of equal value. A good deal of discrimination is called for – together with an active sense of humour.

5 THURSDAY ☿ *Moon Age Day 1 Moon Sign Cancer*

Communication becomes all-important, and the present position of the Moon encourages you to mix with a wide cross-section of different people. Everyone has their tale to tell and you should be more than willing to listen. In amongst everything you hear today you can find some genuine pearls of wisdom.

6 FRIDAY ☿ *Moon Age Day 2 Moon Sign Cancer*

Venus assists you to bring even greater stability to your financial doings and to seek out the genuine bargains that eluded you across the last couple of weeks. How pleased you will now be if you took the astrological advice on offer and kept your purse or wallet firmly closed. Plan now for some travel later.

7 SATURDAY ☿ *Moon Age Day 3 Moon Sign Leo*

You may well decide to stay at home and to allow others to visit you this weekend. All the same you needn't isolate yourself and can afford to mix freely with family members, friends and neighbours. In amongst the mix you need as much familiarity and personal support as you can get – particularly if you feel slightly insecure.

8 SUNDAY ☿ *Moon Age Day 4 Moon Sign Leo*

You can show yourself to be very disciplined and a good worker, even if you have to look hard on a Sunday to find anything much to do. Aside from domestic chores you might have to be quite inventive and may well get a great deal of pleasure from entertaining. Long journeys are not likely today, at a time when you can still get the world to come to you.

9 MONDAY ☿ *Moon Age Day 5 Moon Sign Leo*

You may inadvertently create an atmosphere of tension around yourself, encouraged by the present position of the planet Mars in your solar chart. You can best avoid the eventuality by refusing to become involved in schemes or any sort of secrecy. The more open you are today with everyone, the better life will pan out.

10 TUESDAY ☿ *Moon Age Day 6 Moon Sign Virgo*

A boost to your ego is on offer, maybe as a result of the things others are saying to you, but wherever it comes from you should be feeling quite pleased with yourself before the day is out. You can certainly cut a dash in social situations and as usual you manage to be elegant, often without doing much to try.

11 WEDNESDAY ☿ *Moon Age Day 7 Moon Sign Virgo*

The focus is now on practical matters, and you might have so much you want to do today that it is very unlikely everything will be completed to your satisfaction. Perhaps you should try to achieve less. At least that way you can be happy with what gets finished and won't end up slightly frustrated.

12 THURSDAY ☿ *Moon Age Day 8 Moon Sign Libra*

You would be wise to avoid making any rash impulse purchases for the moment. Venus can encourage a tendency to splash out too freely, maybe on things you don't need or which you could get cheaper elsewhere. The luxury-loving side of your nature is to the fore and this is a part of your nature that sometimes has to be kept under control.

13 FRIDAY ☿ *Moon Age Day 9 Moon Sign Libra*

Think carefully about ideas put forward by those close to you. They may be well-intentioned, but they are also impractical or even downright impossible! It's up to you to put them back on course, though this might not be very easy. A mixture of diplomacy and firmness is probably the best way forward.

14 SATURDAY ☿ *Moon Age Day 10 Moon Sign Scorpio*

The lunar low arrives, and although there isn't much you can do about the fact, you can nullify any negative effects by simply slowing down a little. It doesn't matter how much you try to get on today, the trends are not supportive. Realising this fact and relaxing is nine-tenths of the battle.

15 SUNDAY ☿ *Moon Age Day 11   Moon Sign Scorpi*

Some Taurus subjects could simply feel exhausted today but at leas
if you do you can be reassured that this is a very temporary situation
If you've been working very hard in one way or another, there i
nothing to say you should keep pushing, especially on a Sunday. D
something different and you should feel on top of the world.

16 MONDAY ☿ *Moon Age Day 12   Moon Sign Scorpi*

Not the best start to any week, since the lunar low is still aroun
during the first part of the day. It's worth allowing others to mak
some of the running at work, whilst you sit back and think thing
through. You can get more or less back to normal by the afternoo
and then get to grips with an important task that might have bee
delayed.

17 TUESDAY ☿ *Moon Age Day 13   Moon Sign Sagittari*

Your home life might be best described as inconsistent whilst Mar
remains in your solar fourth house. Maybe relatives are rather tetch
or inclined to argue simply for the sake of doing so. There could b
some comfort in retiring into a little corner of your own an
allowing others to spat amongst themselves.

18 WEDNESDAY ☿ *Moon Age Day 14   Moon Sign Sagittari*

Trends encourage you to focus your effort today on practica
matters and efforts you are making to get on better in a materia
sense. If relationships figure less in your thinking than might usuall
be the case, this is only because you have your hands full in othe
ways and don't have too much time for personal commitment.

19 THURSDAY ☿ *Moon Age Day 15   Moon Sign Capricor*

A friend or colleague can put you in touch with broader issues, an
all social contacts at the moment have an element of the weird an
the wonderful. A strange period begins to open up for you but i
has potential to be quite entertaining and even intriguing. Rule
and regulations could easily get on your nerves at the moment.

20 FRIDAY ☿ *Moon Age Day 16 Moon Sign Capricorn*

Your powers of attraction are strengthened thanks to Venus, which has now moved into your solar third house. This is a particularly good planetary position as far as you are concerned. Venus is your own ruling planet and when it sits in the third house it can make it easier for you to verbalise your emotions and even to find new love.

21 SATURDAY *Moon Age Day 17 Moon Sign Capricorn*

This can be a fairly satisfying day and is a time during which money matters are easier to address than might have seemed to be the case in the recent past. Quick successes are available, and you may now be inclined to speak your mind and to ignore the possible consequences. You can make people marvel at your present wit!

22 SUNDAY *Moon Age Day 18 Moon Sign Aquarius*

You have scope to shine with ingenious plans and to be very motivated now. There are plenty of good ideas about, so why not put some of them into practice? Maybe most important of all at the moment is your ability to get other people working on your behalf. You have to do very little except encourage and collect the gains.

23 MONDAY *Moon Age Day 19 Moon Sign Aquarius*

Trends offer you a good day to talk to someone special and to make new attachments from what were previously only acquaintances. If someone thinks you are wonderful, you can persuade them to tell you so under present planetary trends. How you react to all the compliments remains to be seen. Try to do more than simply blushing.

24 TUESDAY *Moon Age Day 20 Moon Sign Pisces*

Even if things are working out well as far as the wider world is concerned, there may still be a few minor problems to deal with at home. Set aside some time to address these and don't avoid issues simply because you don't care for the look of them. A few wise words right now can work wonders.

25 WEDNESDAY   *Moon Age Day 21   Moon Sign Pisce*

The Moon brings a favourable trend socially and enhances you present ability to shine like a beacon when in company. A particula offer may be available to you at any time now and it would be rathe foolish to ignore its implications. Whatever boosts your ego i worth listening to now because it could well be true.

26 THURSDAY   *Moon Age Day 22   Moon Sign Pisce*

A period of quiet solitude would be no bad thing for today. This i not to suggest that you lock yourself up for the whole of the day On the contrary, you can spend at least part of your time out there in the wider world. It's just that you can also gain from taking an hour or two to yourself, in order to meditate.

27 FRIDAY   *Moon Age Day 23   Moon Sign Aries*

Independence is gradually becoming your middle name. You probably won't take kindly to being told what to do, and Taurus can be very stubborn when necessary. The fact is that you think you know best for most of the time at the moment and you might be very anxious to follow your own notions to their ultimate conclusions.

28 SATURDAY   *Moon Age Day 24   Moon Sign Aries*

There is still a strong mixture of quiet contemplation and positive actions. This might seem perfectly natural to you but might well confuse some of the people with whom you are mixing today. Your partner deserves more of your time than they have been enjoying over the last few days, so why not put a little attention in that direction?

29 SUNDAY   *Moon Age Day 25   Moon Sign Taurus*

The lunar high returns and brings with it some of the most important incentives that the month has offered. A little frustration could be the result because you may not be able to do exactly what you would wish in a practical sense on a Sunday. Fortunately you can also get into the right frame of mind to go out and have some fun.

30 MONDAY
Moon Age Day 26   Moon Sign Taurus

Enterprising ideas come thick and fast and it may be all you can do to keep up with your own thought processes. Don't be too quick to jump to conclusions and try to follow through once you have started a particular course of action. All in all you have what it takes to make this one of the most progressive days for quite some time.

♉

July

2008

1 TUESDAY
Moon Age Day 27   Moon Sign Gemini

Pleasant conversations and congenial company are particularly important to you at the moment. Make the most of that third-house Venus by mixing freely with urbane and witty people, and find comfortable places to occupy. If ever there was a time for strawberries and champagne you have found it at the start of this July.

2 WEDNESDAY
Moon Age Day 28   Moon Sign Gemini

Self-expression is now the key to happiness so it is worth searching for just the right words to tell others how you feel. If you aren't very keen to get involved in anything dirty or unsavoury, one option is to let others do some of the less pleasant jobs. The only problem is that they might complain about the fact!

3 THURSDAY
Moon Age Day 0   Moon Sign Cancer

Now you can afford to entertain some very big ideas. Your mental powers are strong, and positive thinking is not only important but vital if you really want to get on well. If most of today is spent with practical situations, it's true to say that love and romance especially are inclined to take a back seat. It's worth trying to redress the balance later.

4 FRIDAY
Moon Age Day 1   Moon Sign Cancer

Any family issue that arises at this time could come to take on an importance far beyond what seems either necessary or prudent. Once you have dealt with this issue you will be free to pursue your own course, but even then there are likely to be frequent little issues cropping up that demand your time and cause frustration.

5 SATURDAY   *Moon Age Day 2   Moon Sign Leo*

Your strength lies in positive interactions with loved ones. This may well be because the arrival of the weekend is giving you slightly more time to please yourself and to concentrate on relationships. Try to ring the changes in a social sense, even if it is only by going somewhere different for a few hours.

6 SUNDAY   *Moon Age Day 3   Moon Sign Leo*

Trends now offer you plenty of reason to be cheerful. It looks as though Lady Luck is favouring you more than might usually be the case and you can afford to take the odd calculated risk because your intuition is so strong. In a domestic sense it is very important that you avoid that Taurean tendency of trying to keep up with the Joneses.

7 MONDAY   *Moon Age Day 4   Moon Sign Virgo*

It's possible for you to achieve a certain amount of ongoing success where money matters are concerned and you have what it takes to be in the right place for a bargain or two this week. Your attitude is good and people are certainly keeping an eye on you. That means that working Taureans could go for advancement of some sort.

8 TUESDAY   *Moon Age Day 5   Moon Sign Virgo*

Colleagues or friends can bring out the best in you at the moment and you can relish the attention of people you find interesting and stimulating. It's all about your mind around this time and your intellectual capacities seem somehow increased. The more high-flying the company, the better you should enjoy the experience.

9 WEDNESDAY   *Moon Age Day 6   Moon Sign Libra*

The Sun remains in your solar third house, which can help you to increase your verbal dexterity and to communicate with all manner of people. That's good because you are not only talking, you are listening a good deal too. Everyone has their tale to tell and what they have to say can be very useful.

10 THURSDAY
Moon Age Day 7   Moon Sign Libra

Though your personal magnetism remains high, you need to be cautious not to be overconfident and to blow one or two of your best plans simply because you aren't careful enough. Your approach with family members and even friends can be rather too positive, and you might need to tone your nature down a little.

11 FRIDAY
Moon Age Day 8   Moon Sign Libra

As the days go on your over-exuberance becomes less significant because the Moon is rapidly approaching Scorpio, bringing your lunar low for the month. That comes later today but in the meantime you can achieve an active and enterprising start to this Friday. It's worth getting a few things sorted now that you can deal with more positively next week.

12 SATURDAY
Moon Age Day 9   Moon Sign Scorpio

This may not be the most outgoing or exciting weekend you have ever known, but you can make sure it has its good points. For one thing you have more scope to rest and relax which, considering the pace of your life recently, has to be a good thing. At the same time you might have more time to listen to your partner or family members.

13 SUNDAY
Moon Age Day 10   Moon Sign Scorpio

This is probably not one of the best days of the month for you when it comes to capitalising on opportunities. It might be better not to try and to simply drift with the tide for a while. There is no harm in taking a short holiday from life, and by tomorrow you can get right back on course, as well as being less stressed.

14 MONDAY
Moon Age Day 11   Moon Sign Sagittarius

A good dose of positive thinking can now have a tremendous bearing on your life and the general circumstances that surround you. Because you are so go-getting you needn't let a single opportunity pass you by. Even if nothing particularly special is happening, you are in a position to handle what is around much more successfully.

15 TUESDAY   *Moon Age Day 12   Moon Sign Sagittarius*

Mars has now moved into your solar fifth house, which assists you to expand your ego. Fortunately the position of the Sun is such that you also have an enhanced sense of humour. It shouldn't bother you at all to be teased, and on the contrary you can see the funny side of almost anything you do. You can make this a very happy period.

16 WEDNESDAY *Moon Age Day 13   Moon Sign Sagittarius*

In amongst the very busy pattern your life is taking, don't be afraid to find moments to enjoy family life and all it offers. Today could be such a period and is a time when your ruling planet Venus has much to offer you. With loved ones you can be quieter and spend as much time listening as you do talking.

17 THURSDAY   *Moon Age Day 14   Moon Sign Capricorn*

All in all, trends bring restlessness at present and you may not take at all kindly to being restricted in any way. Even so, some lively intellectual activity and a change of scenery would definitely be in order around now. Holidays may be in the offing, but even if they are not you need to ring the changes somehow.

18 FRIDAY   *Moon Age Day 15   Moon Sign Capricorn*

In terms of communication this has potential to be a very hectic phase, and this applies as much to your social life as it may to your work. If someone you haven't met for quite some time comes back into your life, they may offer the chance of a replay of situations from the past. It's worth keeping one eye on the future though.

19 SATURDAY   *Moon Age Day 16   Moon Sign Aquarius*

Increased mental energy encourages you to keep a thousand different things in your mind this weekend and the best place to view everything is from a different perspective. Once again you might have the urge to travel. It doesn't matter whether you find yourself at the top of a remote hill or by the sea. The change matters.

20 SUNDAY
Moon Age Day 17   Moon Sign Aquarius

Positive thinking really can make it so – at least it can if you also put in that extra bit of effort that makes all the difference. There is also a chance you might meet someone who can be of real importance to you, and that what they have to tell you will lead to a sea change in attitude on your behalf.

21 MONDAY
Moon Age Day 18   Moon Sign Aquarius

There is a very harmonious period on offer, especially amongst family members and friends. You may decide to let romance rear its head to a greater extent and it is clear that you have what it takes to make your partner very happy indeed. Little chores that you don't relish can be got out of the way in a fraction of the usual time they take.

22 TUESDAY
Moon Age Day 19   Moon Sign Pisces

A marvellous mental boost is available when it comes to conversation and intellectual exchanges of any sort. You can show yourself to be as refined as Taurus often is and should relish pleasant surroundings. It is also an ideal time to think about making changes to your home at any time during this period.

23 WEDNESDAY
Moon Age Day 20   Moon Sign Pisces

Trends suggest you could be caught out now by an issue that comes directly from the past. However, even if you did not approach the matter very well first time around, now you are in a much better position to handle it successfully. Don't be afraid to ask for some advice regarding any matters you do not totally understand yourself.

24 THURSDAY
Moon Age Day 21   Moon Sign Aries

You are not entering a two-day period during which a little solitude is not only possible, it is also advisable. The Moon occupies your solar twelfth house and this encourages more contemplation, and puts an edge on your intuition. You can make others marvel at your ability to look ahead and to see things so clearly.

25 FRIDAY
Moon Age Day 22   Moon Sign Aries

Even if you communicate well with friends, you might prefer to stay away from individuals you find either contentious or troublesome to your spirit. With everything to play for in a material sense you might still opt for quiet and contemplation. You know instinctively that this is not exactly the right time during which to act.

26 SATURDAY
Moon Age Day 23   Moon Sign Taurus

Your intuitive and mental powers are stimulated even more as the Moon returns to your zodiac sign. The lunar high this time coincides with the weekend, so much of your energy may well be given to social and family pursuits. This would be the very best time of the year to be thinking about taking a holiday.

27 SUNDAY
Moon Age Day 24   Moon Sign Taurus

Opportunity is certainly knocking on your door repeatedly around this time but there are so many possibilities about that it might be difficult to follow up every potential gain. In any case you are not too materially minded, and the lunar high is more likely to stimulate your desire for fun in the company of those you love.

28 MONDAY
Moon Age Day 25   Moon Sign Gemini

You can now make use of a real talent for maintaining growth in your life and you show a real appreciation of the finer things that surround you. In a material sense you still have what it takes to make progress, but this is of a very considered sort. Trends don't encourage you to act on impulse as much as was the case earlier this month.

29 TUESDAY
Moon Age Day 26   Moon Sign Gemini

It looks as though this would be a good time to be at home. The Sun has now passed into your solar fourth house, so you are in for a month or so during which domestic considerations are highlighted. Don't be afraid to let a loved one take you down memory lane – it's always a happy place to be for you.

119

30 WEDNESDAY   *Moon Age Day 27   Moon Sign Cance*

Right now you can use communication matters to make life bot
interesting and varied. The accent is still on those you know an
love and your association with the world at large is now les
accented. Nevertheless what you hear and see outside of your hom
today may be vital in terms of ordering your future.

31 THURSDAY   *Moon Age Day 28   Moon Sign Cance*

It's a good time to discuss things with family members and especiall
with your partner. Trends assist you to be reasonable in your attitud
and just as willing to listen to another point of view as to push you
own forward. For this reason alone you are more likely to get you
own way, and diplomacy seems to be your middle name now.

August

2008

FRIDAY   Moon Age Day 0   Moon Sign Leo

With the first day of August comes a period during which it is vital to make a good impression with anyone, right from the start. You may need to find reserves within yourself that you didn't really know you possessed, and your energy is heightened under present trends. Just don't push yourself too hard!

SATURDAY   Moon Age Day 1   Moon Sign Leo

You are usually very warm and supportive to those people who are closest to you, but you should also be good when dealing with acquaintances or strangers. Everyone has the right to see the best side of your nature at the moment, and you could be going to tremendous lengths in order to satisfy the needs of a world for which you care deeply.

SUNDAY   Moon Age Day 2   Moon Sign Virgo

Trends suggest that home and family are the issues that count the most with Taurus at the moment, and you have scope to work hard on behalf of those you love. Elements of the past are still likely to play in your mind and you are filled with positive emotions when it comes to expressing your love for others. This can be a warm and happy time.

MONDAY   Moon Age Day 3   Moon Sign Virgo

Matters of the heart have a lot going for them at the moment and the more amorous amongst Taurus subjects can make sure they have a very good time indeed! If you are settled in your personal attachments you might still want to prove just how important your partner is to you, so why not do something unexpected and flamboyant?

121

5 TUESDAY
Moon Age Day 4   Moon Sign Virgo

An ideal day to use family discussions to clear up misunderstanding and to find a better way forward, especially with regard to anyone who has been rather touchy of late. Bringing things out into the open generally is something you will be inclined to do around this time, and it really helps to clear the air.

6 WEDNESDAY
Moon Age Day 5   Moon Sign Libra

With the Moon now in your solar sixth house, you are encouraged to keep very busy today, even if there isn't really anything much to do. You need to feel necessary and even important, so you should be particularly pleased if others notice your contributions. Don't expect too much from colleagues and go it alone at work.

7 THURSDAY
Moon Age Day 6   Moon Sign Libra

Personal plans could receive some setbacks at this stage of the week and in any situation where you are even slightly in doubt it is important to check and then double-check. You can put the more refined side of your nature on show once again, and you may well shy away from doing anything that you consider unsavoury

8 FRIDAY
Moon Age Day 7   Moon Sign Scorpio

Once again personal plans may be difficult as the Moon now enters the zodiac sign of Scorpio and brings you to the lunar low of the month. There are still some very positive planetary positions around and you should be quite well supported in a financial sense. However, you might feel slightly down in the dumps for a few hours.

9 SATURDAY
Moon Age Day 8   Moon Sign Scorpio

A day to guard against sloppy and impractical thinking and to make sure that whatever you do is undertaken properly. You will need to check your own work and that of others because there is a distinct chance that mistakes can be made. Away from the professional scene you can make sure your home life proves more comfortable.

10 SUNDAY   *Moon Age Day 9   Moon Sign Sagittarius*

Away from the lunar low you can now show a probing intuition and an insatiable desire to know what is going on generally in the wide world beyond your own door. Trends encourage you to be active and enterprising, filled with potential new incentives and just raring to have a go at something that has been denied you in the past.

11 MONDAY   *Moon Age Day 10   Moon Sign Sagittarius*

Romantic possibilities of all kinds are now furthered by the position of Venus in your solar chart. You can use this trend to get yourself noticed, and people could find you to be even more attractive than would usually be the case. You might also show a strong desire for luxury and for surroundings that are comfortable and opulent.

12 TUESDAY   *Moon Age Day 11   Moon Sign Sagittarius*

There are potential new social interests on the way. Maybe you have decided to take up some new form of pastime or hobby, or it could be that you simply want to mix with a different group of people. Don't forget that this is August and therefore high summer. Get yourself out of the house. A day trip might prove to be entertaining.

13 WEDNESDAY   *Moon Age Day 12   Moon Sign Capricorn*

Intimacy is called for by the present planetary line-up, encouraging you to stick almost exclusively to those people who figure in your life the most. Outsiders may not get into your little world today and you probably want to be with those you trust. Once again you have the desire to travel, but now in the company of a closed circle.

14 THURSDAY   *Moon Age Day 13   Moon Sign Capricorn*

Venus signals a time of heightened pleasure and a smooth passage as far as romantic matters are concerned. If you are a young Taurean or one who is presently on the lookout for a new relationship, this is the time when you can make things begin to happen. Be prepared to give situations a nudge yourself.

15 FRIDAY
Moon Age Day 14   Moon Sign Aquarius

Change and growth is now forecast in your chart, though it tends to come with a fairly spluttering start. Just because ideas don't turn out right immediately doesn't mean you should abandon them out of hand. The adage 'try and try again' is especially appropriate for Taurus today, and indeed across the next week or so.

16 SATURDAY
Moon Age Day 15   Moon Sign Aquarius

You can be very gregarious now and the present astrological line-up helps to bring out the actor in you. Even if you are not performing on a real stage it seems that life serves the same purpose for you. This is one of the best days of the month both for expressing yourself and for truly understanding what others are about.

17 SUNDAY
Moon Age Day 16   Moon Sign Aquarius

Domestic and family affairs could prove to be rather rewarding right now, though you also show a fairly restless streak and may not want to stick around the house all day, even though it's Sunday. It doesn't much matter where you go because the important thing is to get a change of scenery. You can persuade friends to go along with you.

18 MONDAY
Moon Age Day 17   Moon Sign Pisces

Trends indicate that you may now feel less in control of certain aspects of your life, and this can be an unnerving situation for Taurus. Having to rely heavily on others never pleases you and that is possibly what is taking place at the moment. This is less of a problem if the people helping you out are those who have been friends for many years.

19 TUESDAY
Moon Age Day 18   Moon Sign Pisces

The signs are that you may be spending a lot of time trying to improve things at work, and without much in the way of apparent success. Patience is needed and fortunately that is a commodity you have in buckets. It's worth setting your sights on what you want to achieve and moving slowly towards it. You have what it takes to win out in the end.

20 WEDNESDAY *Moon Age Day 19 Moon Sign Aries*

This would be a good time to evaluate existing romantic attachments and to ask yourself whether they are working out in quite the way you would wish. Now is certainly the moment to speak your mind, even if this means slightly upsetting someone else. Don't let any sort of difficult situation perpetuate.

21 THURSDAY *Moon Age Day 20 Moon Sign Aries*

When it comes to getting things done in a practical or a material sense you might have to push well beyond your normal powers of endurance today if you want real success. Fortunately Taurus is one of the strongest and most resilient of all the zodiac signs. Being made of tough stuff, you can go on and on if necessary.

22 FRIDAY *Moon Age Day 21 Moon Sign Taurus*

The initiative is now with you and the lunar high allows you to go well beyond your usual abilities in almost every way. The most obvious thing about today should be your popularity. People love you so much that they can be persuaded to do almost anything for you, which is why this is definitely the time to ask for anything you really want.

23 SATURDAY *Moon Age Day 22 Moon Sign Taurus*

A period of personal and possibly professional progress is definitely on offer. The working side of things might be somewhat restricted if the weekend is your own, but all this means is that you can push your energy into social and personal projects instead. This is certainly not the right time to be hiding your light under a bushel.

24 SUNDAY *Moon Age Day 23 Moon Sign Gemini*

Trends offer you increased physical energy and tremendous initiative. It's time for Taurus to take command, even if one or two people seem less than happy about the situation. Fortunately you can also be very diplomatic at present so you should be able to get yourself adopted as the natural leader, and without any real argument.

125

25 MONDAY
Moon Age Day 24   Moon Sign Gemini

Work matters could be put under considerable pressure, though not necessarily as a result of anything you are doing yourself. If situations beyond your control arise, these will take some careful thought on your part. Once again you can prove yourself equal to almost any task and shouldn't be short of good ideas.

26 TUESDAY
Moon Age Day 25   Moon Sign Gemini

There are good influences about as far as personal matters are concerned, though friends might be proving slightly difficult to deal with and will require a greater level of understanding. Your best approach is to spend some time with them and try to persuade them to talk about what is troubling them. You can be a great help to your pals today.

27 WEDNESDAY
Moon Age Day 26   Moon Sign Cancer

You seem to need constant stimulation of the mental sort and probably won't be at all happy if you feel you have been shoved into the background in any situation at all. Taurus can afford to be more up-front than ever and can demand to be noticed. In all social situations, with just a little trouble on your part you can shine like the brightest star.

28 THURSDAY
Moon Age Day 27   Moon Sign Cancer

You have scope to enjoy domestic gatherings or family chats today, and trends assist you to move mountains to make life more comfortable for the people you love. There is also great sympathy within you for anyone who has been having a hard time of late, even if these are not individuals you know very well.

29 FRIDAY
Moon Age Day 28   Moon Sign Leo

The Sun is now in your solar fifth house and this brings a month-long period which encourages you to feel good about yourself – and not necessarily in a quiet way. Taurus is not generally given to being brash or outspoken but you have potential to hog the limelight more under present trends – not that this is at all a bad thing.

30 SATURDAY
Moon Age Day 29   Moon Sign Leo

Your love of life is now likely to be stronger than ever. If you channel all the positive planetary influences into present activities you should radiate a natural charm and charisma that others find difficult to ignore. Taureans who might have been down in the dumps for one reason or another can now afford to be feeling more confident.

31 SUNDAY
Moon Age Day 0   Moon Sign Virgo

If you are a weekend worker you can make this a positive time professionally. A spirit of co-operation now exists and this will allow you to come to common answers to past problems. There is also a possibility that you can make friends with someone you definitely didn't care for in the past.

♍ September ⑧
2008

1 MONDAY
Moon Age Day 1   Moon Sign Virgo

Where career matters are at stake you should be quite happy to put in that extra bit of effort that can make all the difference. You can make good things happen in your life generally and you are able to make a positive impression on people who have influence. In short, you can accomplish almost anything you set out to do.

2 TUESDAY
Moon Age Day 2   Moon Sign Libra

Be prepared to show your dynamism and enthusiasm, no matter what you decide to do. You presently have what it takes to do well in situations that might normally cause you some problems. There is a slight tendency at the moment for you to look back to the past, but even this is for a reason – so that you don't make the same mistakes again.

3 WEDNESDAY
Moon Age Day 3   Moon Sign Libra

If you need to get on with your work today, you won't be happy around people who waste time or who create problems rather than solutions. In almost all aspects of life you can show a positive and inspirational face and can use it to gain friends wherever you go. Socially speaking you should also be on top form this week.

4 THURSDAY
Moon Age Day 4   Moon Sign Scorpio

Vitality could be slightly lacking whilst the lunar low is around, but there are so many positive planetary influences surrounding you at the moment, all that is required is a slight slowing of the pace. You should still show a determination to succeed, but should probably avoid taking any drastic action, at least until after the weekend.

128

5 FRIDAY
Moon Age Day 5   Moon Sign Scorpio

There could be a few disappointments to be contended with today, even if these are of a fairly low-key sort. Niggles and annoyances are also possible, and it could be that you are pushing too hard against a relentless tide. One option is to take a few hours to yourself, stop driving forward and simply wait until the Moon moves out of Scorpio.

6 SATURDAY
Moon Age Day 6   Moon Sign Scorpio

Although the lunar low is still around at the beginning of the day, the Moon will soon move on and you can get back to normal. If what you crave most this weekend is excitement, you may well decide to try something you have shied away from in the past. Could it be that funfair ride you have always avoided?

7 SUNDAY
Moon Age Day 7   Moon Sign Sagittarius

Your organisational skills are highlighted, and even other people will naturally turn to you to get things in their own lives sorted out. You often work long and hard on behalf of others and this may be true at present. Perhaps most important today is your fund of good ideas, some of which need to put into action very soon.

8 MONDAY
Moon Age Day 8   Moon Sign Sagittarius

You function best this week when you can find your own space and when you are left to get on with jobs in your own way. What won't work very well are those occasions when you are under the direct gaze of someone else all the time, or when people are constantly checking your work.

9 TUESDAY
Moon Age Day 9   Moon Sign Capricorn

This is a great period for intellectual growth and for interests that bring you into contact with the outside world. You seem to be able to attract like-minded people under present trends and that is partly because of the air of confidence and purposefulness that you are able to give off. Taurus is potentially on a roll at the moment.

10 WEDNESDAY · Moon Age Day 10 · Moon Sign Capricorn

A day to ensure that those who have to deal with you are generally in for a pleasurable experience. There could hardly be a more typical or loveable Taurean than the one you can present to the world at large right now. Not only should you be charming and refined in your attitude, you can also be extremely kind and quick to help anyone.

11 THURSDAY · Moon Age Day 11 · Moon Sign Capricorn

You work better at the moment if you are in control of whatever you are doing. It shouldn't be difficult for you to hand out instructions to others, but it is more of a problem if you have to take the lead from people who don't really seem to know what they are doing. It looks as though a little diplomacy is called for to straighten things out.

12 FRIDAY · Moon Age Day 12 · Moon Sign Aquarius

Taurus is famous for its common sense, but this doesn't always apply where money is concerned. Being an Earth-sign person you can live on a shoestring if you have to, but you do like luxury and that occasionally leads you to spending money you can't really spare. Today might be such a time, and some care is necessary over purchases.

13 SATURDAY · Moon Age Day 13 · Moon Sign Aquarius

A strong creative impulse this weekend can lead you to new interests, and might even encourage you to do something to beautify your surroundings. Today responds best if you find time for family members, particularly ones who have been going through a difficult time. You should also keep up your hectic social life.

14 SUNDAY · Moon Age Day 14 · Moon Sign Pisces

For today at least you will probably fare better when doing things on your own. This is a practical matter and doesn't relate much to social situations, in which you still have scope to co-operate. There is a slight dichotomy about you right now because you can be both gregarious and insular, depending on the circumstances.

15 MONDAY
Moon Age Day 15   Moon Sign Pisces

Trends foster slight impatience at the beginning of this week, but his isn't necessarily a bad thing. You can put everything you have into your work and shouldn't be diverted from a course of action you know to be right. It's possible that someone in your vicinity has news that means very little to them but a great deal to you.

16 TUESDAY
Moon Age Day 16   Moon Sign Aries

This would be a good time to have a few moments to yourself in which to reflect on the way things are going at the moment. The Moon is passing through your solar twelfth house and this is often a quieter time for you. If aspects of the past are playing through your mind, beware of delling on them too much.

17 WEDNESDAY
Moon Age Day 17   Moon Sign Aries

Your diplomatic talents can bring advantages at work, but may also be useful if you are dealing with warring family members or friends who just can't get along with each other. People do listen to you and especially so at the moment during a phase when it is so easy for you to pour oil on almost any troubled water.

18 THURSDAY
Moon Age Day 18   Moon Sign Aries

Although you have what it takes to stand up for yourself, you might still prefer a quieter time if you can find it. That's not a bad thing, because life has potential to get very hectic indeed tomorrow. It's worth clearing the decks for action, especially at work, and also being aware that the weekend ahead is likely to be fast and potentially exciting.

19 FRIDAY
Moon Age Day 19   Moon Sign Taurus

As far as opportunities are concerned you are entering one of the very best phases for some time. The lunar high is supportive and offers you incentives you wouldn't have expected. What is more, you should know how to shine in almost any situation and should be more than ready to take the world by storm, particularly this evening.

20 SATURDAY   *Moon Age Day 20   Moon Sign Tauru.*

This is a potentially dynamic and inspiring period, though it is not without an element of risk. Even if you feel invincible, you are probably more vulnerable than you think. Fortunately Taurus can retain its common sense, even when the planetary influences are so powerful. Excitement can now be your middle name.

21 SUNDAY   *Moon Age Day 21   Moon Sign Gemini*

You really can enjoy contacts and company right now, and probably won't want to spend more time than is necessary on your own. Routines are OK, as long as you can share them with people you find interesting to be around, and you should take any opportunity to dress up and go somewhere exciting, or where you can put your talents on display.

22 MONDAY   *Moon Age Day 22   Moon Sign Gemini*

Having the capacity to put on various roles when necessary, you can now show yourself to be extremely versatile and only too willing to fill in for people if they are out of sorts or indisposed. This ability stands you in good stead because it means you can make sure you are being watched – probably by people who have great influence.

23 TUESDAY   *Moon Age Day 23   Moon Sign Cancer*

Even if you seem to be busier than ever, you can maintain your depth and should have great insights into specific happenings and also into the motivations of those around you. Your intuition verges on the psychic at the moment, and you can use it to reach conclusions that those with whom you mix will find astounding.

24 WEDNESDAY   *Moon Age Day 24   Moon Sign Cancer*

It might not be easy for you to put your finger on sources of tension that are developing at home, but it is worth that extra bit of effort necessary to find out what it really going on. Bringing others round to your point of view shouldn't be hard, and you certainly have what it takes to make your partner or sweetheart very happy indeed

25 THURSDAY ☿ *Moon Age Day 25 Moon Sign Leo*

If you are involved in any sort of task that is essentially physical in nature you should be in your element, but as always you don't take kindly to doing things that you find dirty or unsavoury. A day for getting to grips with issues that have been on your mind for some time, particularly if you can discuss things with family members.

26 FRIDAY ☿ *Moon Age Day 26 Moon Sign Leo*

With Mercury now in your solar sixth house you can show yourself to be especially skilled at using your mind in an analytical way. Why not put this to use regarding issues of financial security and with regard to all practical matters that will benefit from a deeper investigation? You can be a real Sherlock Holmes at the moment.

27 SATURDAY ☿ *Moon Age Day 27 Moon Sign Virgo*

The weekend offers you scope to pick up any sort of information, whether it turns out to be useful or not. Indulging in gossip is probably something you do without thinking, and you might be more attracted than usual to the superficial elements of life. That's fine, because you can't show your depth all the time.

28 SUNDAY ☿ *Moon Age Day 28 Moon Sign Virgo*

You should be able to find plenty of support when you need it, and this is especially true with regard to good friends and family members. When it comes to romance you have what it takes to make the most amazing impression – perhaps sometimes when you don't intend to do so. Don't be surprised if things get a little steamy!

29 MONDAY ☿ *Moon Age Day 29 Moon Sign Libra*

This has potential to be a fairly constructive period in a practical sense and a time during which you can turn your hand to almost anything. Taurus is now so adaptable that you are being actively sought out by many people, and it might be difficult for you to keep track of the situation. You may have to be more selective than usual.

30 TUESDAY ☿ *Moon Age Day 0   Moon Sign Libra*

Your keen sense of organisation is never sharper than it is at the moment. You can gain support for your actions from people who are in positions of authority, and you are able to mix easily and freely with just about anyone. A quieter time is on offer, so if there is anything positive that needs to be done, do it today or tomorrow.

October

2008

1 WEDNESDAY ☿ *Moon Age Day 1 Moon Sign Libra*

The first day of October can be active, enterprising and sometimes quite surprising in what it throws into your path. If by the evening some of the drive you have been maintaining starts to diminish, you might decide to slump in front of the television. A quieter spell probably turns out to be no bad thing.

2 THURSDAY ☿ *Moon Age Day 2 Moon Sign Scorpio*

The lunar low is best served by keeping things as simple as you can and life could take on a rather 'so-so' quality for the next couple of days. This is not to say that you fail to make any headway at all, merely that you do better if you tackle one job at once, which is probably not what you have been doing across the last few days.

3 FRIDAY ☿ *Moon Age Day 3 Moon Sign Scorpio*

If there are impediments to your progress at the moment, there may not be very much you can do to remove them. All in all it would be better to avoid taking on too much and to consolidate what you already have. Rest and recuperation are in order, together with spending quiet time in the company of someone who is dear to you.

4 SATURDAY ☿ *Moon Age Day 4 Moon Sign Sagittarius*

Mars remains in your solar sixth house, and from a practical point of view this planetary position allows you to stay on your toes. The lunar low has now gone and you can once again show yourself to be both positive and quite dynamic in your attitude. Stand by to make a few gains you didn't expect – and one or two of them could be financial.

5 SUNDAY ☿ *Moon Age Day 5   Moon Sign Sagittarius*

With the Sun now also in your solar sixth house you could well begin to develop a sort of perfectionism that is fairly unique to Taurus. Second best probably will not do, and others may have to fall over themselves in order to get things right for you. Maybe you are being just a little too fussy, but woe-betide anyone who says so!

6 MONDAY ☿ *Moon Age Day 6   Moon Sign Sagittarius*

An exciting and adventurous period lies before you this week. There are some really good planetary influences, all of which are urging you onwards towards new incentives and activities. With no time to hang around you can afford to show the world who is boss right now, and few should stand in your way.

7 TUESDAY ☿ *Moon Age Day 7   Moon Sign Capricorn*

You function well when it comes to looking after your own interests, especially in a financial sense. However, it is quite important at the moment that you do not allow your Taurean fondness for detail to get in your way at a time when a broad overview is far more useful. You can obtain any help you need from colleagues.

8 WEDNESDAY ☿ *Moon Age Day 8   Moon Sign Capricorn*

This could be a very confusing and tense time as far as your personal life is concerned, particularly if you fail to look at things in an objective and honest manner. You could easily be worrying about something without any evidence or justification, and that means dissipating otherwise useful energy to no real purpose.

9 THURSDAY ☿ *Moon Age Day 9   Moon Sign Aquarius*

Progress in your career depends on your ability to think down completely new channels. Taurus can certainly be on the ball at the moment but there is a tendency for you to sometimes get stuck in your way of thinking. The more revolutionary you are at present, the greater is the chance that you can get the world at large to take notice.

10 FRIDAY ☿ *Moon Age Day 10*   *Moon Sign Aquarius*

Make the most of a good period for romance, perhaps by sweeping someone completely off their feet. Social relationships should also be very good and will offer you the chance of new friendships, one or two of which might endure for a very long time. This is not to suggest that you ignore old friends, all of whom remain important.

11 SATURDAY ☿ *Moon Age Day 11*   *Moon Sign Aquarius*

Trends encourage you to look towards your pals for a good time this weekend. Formal situations are not significant and rather you can make up your mind as you go along when it comes to enjoyment. The more spontaneous you are, the greater is the chance that you make this one of those very special times that cannot be planned.

12 SUNDAY ☿   *Moon Age Day 12*   *Moon Sign Pisces*

Your critical faculties are excellent and it would take someone very clever indeed to pull the wool over your eyes at the moment. You might decide this is an ideal time for looking at and signing documents of any sort, and for embarking on a new project that is going to demand a great deal of your time and attention in the weeks ahead.

13 MONDAY ☿   *Moon Age Day 13*   *Moon Sign Pisces*

There are signs that you may be too easily distracted at the start of this working week, and for that you can thank the present position of the Moon. Today and tomorrow represent a period when you can rely more on the good offices of colleagues and friends, whilst you take a short break from being quite as organised as you have been.

14 TUESDAY ☿   *Moon Age Day 14*   *Moon Sign Aries*

Romantic and social activities can represent a welcome diversion, especially if you are not in the mood to commit yourself exclusively to work. This would be an excellent time to bury the hatchet in any long-standing disagreement or row, and you have what it takes to play the honest broker for others.

15 WEDNESDAY ☿   *Moon Age Day 15   Moon Sign Aries*

Someone you haven't seen for a very long time could now crop up in your life again, possibly by accident. This situation could please you no end and it isn't out of the question that this will be a friend who was once very dear to you. Times change, but the basic nature of people rarely does, as you now have a chance to discover.

16 THURSDAY ☿   *Moon Age Day 16   Moon Sign Taurus*

You work best now when at the centre of lots of activity. The hotter the situation, the better you should enjoy it, and the cut and thrust of life is what can keep you really busy whilst the lunar high is around. Most important of all at present is your ability to get through or around problems that once seemed impossible to solve.

17 FRIDAY   *Moon Age Day 17   Moon Sign Taurus*

This is the time to push boundaries and to try things out before you decide you are not equal to the task. You can achieve victories now that would have seemed absolutely impossible just a short while ago and shouldn't be at all fazed by any sort of opposition. Taurus can afford to be the fearless bull at the moment!

18 SATURDAY   *Moon Age Day 18   Moon Sign Gemini*

Personal relationships and partnerships of all sorts can now offer much more than you bargained for, though generally in a very positive sense. Your powers of attraction are clearly very strong at the moment so don't be afraid to use them to your own advantage. Just don't lead someone up the garden path romantically.

19 SUNDAY   *Moon Age Day 19   Moon Sign Gemini*

The Moon in your solar third house contributes to a period that fires your curiosity in all sorts of ways. You may now decide you want to know what makes everything tick, and might be turning over every stone as you mosey down the path of life. The result might be one or two real surprises and the odd truly delightful situation.

20 MONDAY   *Moon Age Day 20   Moon Sign Cancer*

You have a very fertile mind at the best of times but now it can be truly active. Intuition is strong and you can afford to back your hunches to a much greater extent than has been the case in the very recent past. Life is now much more about feelings than evidence, though this might be hard for some Taureans to appreciate.

21 TUESDAY   *Moon Age Day 21   Moon Sign Cancer*

Your administrative talents are especially well starred at present, so if there is something that needs organising, now is the time to get cracking. The same is generally true at home, where you have scope to get things organised ahead of the upcoming winter. Taurus can be a bit of a squirrel and likes to get things comfortable!

22 WEDNESDAY   *Moon Age Day 22   Moon Sign Leo*

At this time the focus is clearly on your personal life, and even if you remain generally busy in a practical sense, it's worth spending time in the company of your partner, sorting things out and proving the depth of your affection. All this effort will certainly not be wasted and there is great love coming back in your direction.

23 THURSDAY   *Moon Age Day 23   Moon Sign Leo*

The trends of yesterday continue, helping you to make this a rewarding and happy time when in the company of loved ones. This is not to suggest that your efforts out there in the wider world are diminished, but merely spending time sorting out more personal aspects of your life can work wonders. Younger people could figure significantly now.

24 FRIDAY   *Moon Age Day 24   Moon Sign Virgo*

You have the ability to think and plan on your feet and Mercury, now in your solar sixth house, certainly helps with this regard. What you come up with now should be useful to all concerned and is certainly a benefit to your friends. Trends support selfless acts, and perhaps almost everything you do is for someone else.

139

25 SATURDAY   *Moon Age Day 25   Moon Sign Virgo*

Your strength lies in getting people to notice you this weekend, mainly because of the positive way you express yourself. It is easy to make people feel important and to encourage them to work hard on your behalf. Routines don't appeal, and it's worth ringing the changes whenever possible. A late holiday might be in order.

26 SUNDAY   *Moon Age Day 26   Moon Sign Virgo*

Your diplomatic and interpersonal skills have rarely been better favoured, and it shouldn't be hard to get onside with just about anyone under present trends. Be prepared to use this to approach someone who has really caused you problems in the past, turning difficulties into opportunities. Another strong social day with the possibility of travel.

27 MONDAY   *Moon Age Day 27   Moon Sign Libra*

Handling a heavy workload may not bother you at all as this week gets started, though this situation can change significantly as the days go on, so make the most of this positive beginning. By all means clear the decks for actions that come at the far end of the week, but don't plan anything too strenuous for Wednesday or Thursday.

28 TUESDAY   *Moon Age Day 28   Moon Sign Libra*

Trends assist you to remain productive and capable, though it's possible that one or two people are failing to be quite as helpful or even civil as you might expect. The fault could be on their side, but there is just a chance you are not quite as diplomatic now as was the case only a few days ago. A day to show your compassion and concern.

29 WEDNESDAY   *Moon Age Day 0   Moon Sign Scorpio*

Basically the lunar low brings a slight downer of a period and a time during which you might decide to take a well-earned break. Even if not everything you do is going wrong, it might be hard to make any significant headway and it might be best not to push yourself at all. Support can be gained from colleagues and friends.

30 THURSDAY   *Moon Age Day 1   Moon Sign Scorpio*

Today could be slightly characterised by confusion – that is, unless you do one job at once and think things through carefully before you commit yourself to anything at all. Fortunately you can make sure there is a great deal of good humour about too, together with the company of people who have the ability to make you laugh out loud.

31 FRIDAY   *Moon Age Day 2   Moon Sign Sagittarius*

The lunar low is now well and truly out of the way and Friday offers more in the way of innovation and inspiration. Your best approach is to split your time between practical necessities and those things you actively want to do. You can show yourself to be quite sporting and more than able to win through in solo or team situations.

1 SATURDAY   *Moon Age Day 3   Moon Sign Sagittariu*

The changes you make to your finances can give you more ease and comfort in your surroundings, though this is likely to be a gradual process that takes place across the next few weeks. For now there i scope to be happy. Taurus may well be in the mood for a spot o shopping or a trip to visit relatives or friends.

2 SUNDAY   *Moon Age Day 4   Moon Sign Sagittariu*

A boost to your general level of optimism is possible courtesy of the Moon. If your sense of personal freedom is strong, there won't be much that could hold you back when it comes to pleasing yourself on this November Sunday. A day to leave any worries on the back burne whilst you set out to explore a world that changes all the time.

3 MONDAY   *Moon Age Day 5   Moon Sign Capricorn*

There is a testing phase on the way for your partnerships, whethe these are of a personal or a professional sort. If you are operating more as a solo agent for the moment, that might be part of what i causing the potential problems. This would be out of character because you are usually so good at sharing.

4 TUESDAY   *Moon Age Day 6   Moon Sign Capricorn*

The Sun in your solar seventh house can act as a boost to friendship and nullifies to some extent the position of Mars. Group-relate matters look much livelier and potentially more successful than they did yesterday, and you might also be much more willing to allow someone else to make a few of the major decisions.

5 WEDNESDAY   *Moon Age Day 7   Moon Sign Aquarius*

Although there is presently little scope for shortcuts to success, this fact needn't bother you too much. Taurus is used to working hard for what it wants, and whilst others tire easily, you can keep going no matter what. Some Taureans might look a little fragile, but nothing could be further from the truth.

6 THURSDAY   *Moon Age Day 8   Moon Sign Aquarius*

You could benefit greatly today from getting together with others and discussing almost anything under the sun. Some of the best answers you find at the moment can come as a result of these discussions, and if you are in a very 'think tank' mentality, the more people you draw into your circle, the better the results you can achieve.

7 FRIDAY   *Moon Age Day 9   Moon Sign Aquarius*

Some Taurus subjects may now decide on significant changes as far as personal relationships are concerned. This is a period stimulated by your ruling planet Venus, which presently occupies your solar eighth house of change. Relationships may take on a new and better feel, or new ones could be started now.

8 SATURDAY   *Moon Age Day 10   Moon Sign Pisces*

Paradoxically for those of you who do not work at the weekend, today offers some of the very best professional prospects of the week. You can afford to be quite decisive now and not leave anything to chance. Domestic prospects are very slightly less rosy, particularly if those around you are tetchy or inclined to be over-critical about something.

9 SUNDAY   *Moon Age Day 11   Moon Sign Pisces*

Partnerships are to the fore, especially if you are trying hard to bring someone round to a point of view that seems quite self-evident to you. No matter how hard you try, you may have difficulty persuading someone to follow your lead, and finding a compromise may be your best response.

10 MONDAY
Moon Age Day 12   Moon Sign Aries

With the Moon passing through the quiet solar twelfth house, the impact you make on life is apt to be rather less positive or even noticeable than has been the case. This might not be an entirely bad thing, because there are potentially even busier times ahead, and there could be significant gains from standing still and taking stock.

11 TUESDAY
Moon Age Day 13   Moon Sign Aries

Venus can help you to make personal relationships far more rewarding today and brings a phase during which you can find time to listen to what those closest to you are actually saying. Much of what you hear now seems to make eminent sense, and you can use it to make progress in areas that might have been a problem for while.

12 WEDNESDAY
Moon Age Day 14   Moon Sign Taurus

The arrival of the lunar high encourages your individuality, and you needn't stay in the background. Wherever there is action, that is where you should choose to be, because Taurus is now about as dynamic and driving as it is possible for the zodiac sign to be. Getting your own way could prove to be relatively easy.

13 THURSDAY
Moon Age Day 15   Moon Sign Taurus

You can now show quite unusual ways of responding to what life offers you, with the result that you are living your life in a fairly unique way. The attraction you have for others isn't at all in doubt, and you can turn heads wherever you go. This period isn't all about work because from a social point of view you have what it takes to sizzle!

14 FRIDAY
Moon Age Day 16   Moon Sign Gemini

The big lesson to learn today is that you need to be careful about exerting a possessive influence on those close to you. It may not be the right way forward to try and make them change to suit your wants or needs. In any case you will be more likely to have a positive influence on them if you allow them to decide for themselves.

15 SATURDAY — *Moon Age Day 17 — Moon Sign Gemini*

If you are feeling slightly insecure at the moment, this is part of the reason why you are inclined to be somewhat jealous or possessive. This is the less favourable face of Taurus and something you need to fight against in any situation. With a little effort you can become more giving and understanding, which is the Taurus everyone loves.

16 SUNDAY — *Moon Age Day 18 — Moon Sign Cancer*

Changeability is an effect of the Moon in your third house, but its position there also encourages you to talk, particularly about emotional and personal matters. Your thinking processes needn't be fixed at the moment and you may well exhibit more of a butterfly mentality than would usually be the case.

17 MONDAY — *Moon Age Day 19 — Moon Sign Cancer*

A period of some mental pressure is possible at this time, particularly if you have so many choices to make. Try not to dwell too much on specific issues and allow your intuition to be at least part of your guide. This is because your usual common sense might not be enough to get you the answers you need.

18 TUESDAY — *Moon Age Day 20 — Moon Sign Leo*

Now is a time to be widening your horizons, and it would also be an excellent period for making any sort of journey. Why not contact people you don't see all that often? They can bring with them an entirely different way of looking at issues you thought you had put to bed some time ago.

19 WEDNESDAY — *Moon Age Day 21 — Moon Sign Leo*

Good communications with relatives and with your partner will probably be needed today if you are to solve a slight problem or series of problems at home. There is a great deal to be said at the moment for sticking with a few routines and also for allowing others to take some of the strain.

27 SATURDAY   Moon Age Day 0   Moon Sign Capricorn

If you are involved in discussions today, you could find that the people around you are proving to be more argumentative than you may have expected. You need to keep your patience and to explain yourself as fully as you can. If things still don't go the way you want, you must either compromise or else do your own thing.

28 SUNDAY   Moon Age Day 1   Moon Sign Capricorn

Along comes a busy period with a definite tendency towards movement and travel. You may decide to visit relatives at a distance or else enliven the holidays by going somewhere special. Whatever you decide to do today it should be something that is as far away from normal routines as you can possibly manage.

29 MONDAY   Moon Age Day 2   Moon Sign Capricorn

Be open to new input today and allow yourself the right to change your mind if you know instinctively it is necessary to do so. This might involve you in some fairly deep discussions in order to explain yourself, but you can use your silver tongue at the moment and shouldn't have any trouble getting others to agree with you.

RISING SIGNS FOR TAURUS

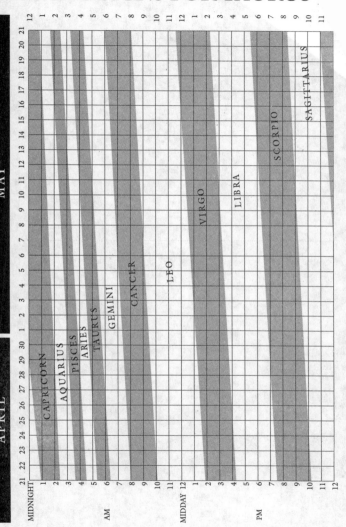

THE ZODIAC, PLANETS AND CORRESPONDENCES

The Earth revolves around the Sun once every calendar year, so when viewed from Earth the Sun appears in a different part of the sky as the year progresses. In astrology, these parts of the sky are divided into the signs of the zodiac and this means that the signs are organised in a circle. The circle begins with Aries and ends with Pisces.

Taking the zodiac sign as a starting point, astrologers then work with all the positions of planets, stars and many other factors to calculate horoscopes and birth charts and tell us what the stars have in store for us.

The table below shows the planets and Elements for each of the signs of the zodiac. Each sign belongs to one of the four Elements: Fire, Air, Earth or Water. Fire signs are creative and enthusiastic; Air signs are mentally active and thoughtful; Earth signs are constructive and practical; Water signs are emotional and have strong feelings.

It also shows the metals and gemstones associated with, or corresponding with, each sign. The correspondence is made when a metal or stone possesses properties that are held in common with a particular sign of the zodiac.

Finally, the table shows the opposite of each star sign – this is the opposite sign in the astrological circle.

Placed	Sign	Symbol	Element	Planet	Metal	Stone	Opposite
1	Aries	Ram	Fire	Mars	Iron	Bloodstone	Libra
2	Taurus	Bull	Earth	Venus	Copper	Sapphire	Scorpio
3	Gemini	Twins	Air	Mercury	Mercury	Tiger's Eye	Sagittarius
4	Cancer	Crab	Water	Moon	Silver	Pearl	Capricorn
5	Leo	Lion	Fire	Sun	Gold	Ruby	Aquarius
6	Virgo	Maiden	Earth	Mercury	Mercury	Sardonyx	Pisces
7	Libra	Scales	Air	Venus	Copper	Sapphire	Aries
8	Scorpio	Scorpion	Water	Pluto	Plutonium	Jasper	Taurus
9	Sagittarius	Archer	Fire	Jupiter	Tin	Topaz	Gemini
10	Capricorn	Goat	Earth	Saturn	Lead	Black Onyx	Cancer
11	Aquarius	Waterbearer	Air	Uranus	Uranium	Amethyst	Leo
12	Pisces	Fishes	Water	Neptune	Tin	Moonstone	Virgo